Praise for *Consumer Republic*

"[A] persuasive and refreshing defence of brands and the power that consumers can wield over corporations."
– *Winnipeg Free Press*

"*Consumer Republic* marks the beginning of a new age in marketing." – Mitch Joel, author of *Six Pixels of Separation*

"An upbeat message at a time when many people around the world are feeling disempowered by corporate power."
– *The Georgia Straight*

"Leads the way to the world of tomorrow – where consumers and brands cooperate to put an end to senseless consumption. A must-read."
– Rahaf Harfoush, author of *Yes We Did: An Inside Look at How Social Media Built the Obama Brand*

"Clever, often funny, and perceptive of contemporary marketing. An engaging and topical read."
– *The Vancouver Observer*

"*Consumer Republic* is a manual instructing modern consumers on how to take the power position in their relationships with corporations. Readers would be well-advised to pay attention." – *Quill & Quire*

"It is essential we all read this book."
– *The Toowoomba Chronicle*

BRUCE PHILP

CONSUMER REPUBLIC

USING BRANDS TO GET WHAT YOU WANT, MAKE CORPORATIONS BEHAVE, AND MAYBE EVEN SAVE THE WORLD

EMBLEM
McClelland & Stewart

Cloth edition published 2011
Emblem Edition published 2012

Emblem is an imprint of McClelland & Stewart Ltd.
Emblem and colophon are registered trademarks of McClelland & Stewart Ltd.

LIBRARY AND ARCHIVES CANADA CATALOGUING IN PUBLICATION

Philp, Bruce, 1958–
Consumer republic : using brands to get what you want, make corporations behave, and maybe even save the world / Bruce Philp.

Includes bibliographical references and index.
Issued also in electronic format.
ISBN 978-0-7710-7002-0

1. Consumer behavior. 2. Brand choice. 3. Brand name products – Marketing. 4. Social responsibility of business. 5. Sustainable living. I. Title.

HF5415.32.P55 2012   658.8'343   C2011-904264-9

We acknowledge the financial support of the Government of Canada through the Book Publishing Industry Development Program and that of the Government of Ontario through the Ontario Media Development Corporation's Ontario Book Initiative. We further acknowledge the support of the Canada Council for the Arts and the Ontario Arts Council for our publishing program.

Published simultaneously in the United States of America by McClelland & Stewart Ltd., P.O. Box 1030, Plattsburgh, New York 12901

Library of Congress Control Number: 2011931120

Cover art: © Shutterstock.com
Typeset in Sabon by M&S, Toronto
Printed and bound in Canada

McClelland & Stewart Ltd.
75 Sherbourne Street
Toronto, Ontario M5A 2P9
www.mcclelland.com

1 2 3 4 5   16 15 14 13 12

For Linda Ann, who always knows what matters.

"LET US CULTIVATE OUR GARDEN."

VOLTAIRE

CONTENTS

PREFACE

For the last three decades or so, marketing has been my career, much of it spent in advertising and branding as a strategist. My job has been to figure out how to get marketers what they want from you, by getting you what you want from them. Wherever there's common ground between you and those marketers, there's business to be done, and my preoccupation has been to find it.

Through all the years I've spent inside the machine of marketing, a couple of uncomfortable truths about this work have stuck with me, truths that have suddenly taken on more importance as we stare down the barrel of an uncertain future for consumerism and the way we live.

The first is how adversarial the relationship often is between the people who buy things and the organizations they buy them from. It's just odd. In a free market, you would think that creating value and then delivering it to satisfied customers would be a pretty pleasant process. Yet, when you spend time listening to people talk about marketing and corporations, especially in generalities, you're more likely to hear suspicion and hostility in their voices than you will delight. You'd almost think they were talking about governments, given the strong feelings, a strange combination of resentment and high expectations, they seem to hold about corporations. Meanwhile, in the boardrooms of the nation, while you'll rarely encounter corporate types who are actually hostile to their customers, you'll certainly see plenty of wariness. Their world is about what they can get away with – in a product's features, its quality, its price, and where and how it's sold – and it breeds an approach to consumers as circumspect as what you'd take around a stranger's Rottweiler.

The second truth is that the buying public misperceives its power over corporations. We seem to believe we don't have any. Without a doubt, there are situations where we don't have much – there are industries where there isn't enough choice for consumers to have any power, industries where the product being sold is such a commodity that competitors behave more like cartels, and industries that don't do business with ordinary people at all. But mostly, we consumers are, in fact, extremely powerful. The compact that we've collectively had with the corporate world practically since the Industrial Revolution has been a bit like the one that kept the planet from turning into an ashtray during the Cold War: mutual assured destruction. We know, but don't care to admit, that if one of us starves, we both starve. It's a stalemate. Consumers and corporations don't always love or trust each other, but neither of us can afford to walk away from the game.

These are realities I'd accepted without question for a long time, just as you probably have. Now, though, as the world struggles to put its latest – and one of its meanest ever – economic firestorms behind it and casts about for someone to blame, I've begun to wonder if maybe we've been looking at this all wrong.

At the end of the 1980s, there was a surge of environmentalism in Western societies, not unlike what we're experiencing today. Corporations talked seriously about "green marketing" and actually made some tangible moves toward operating this way. Consumers opted in, paying attention to things like unnecessary packaging and engaging in practices like recycling in their homes. Politicians felt compelled to engage in the conversation or else risk being seen as irrelevant by their constituencies. Rather than being a counterculture phenomenon the way it was in the '60s and '70s, being green became part of popular culture, something ordinary people thought about and talked about – and something marketers thought they could exploit to make themselves more attractive to us. Environmentalism became, in the very kindest sense of the word, commercial. There was less heated rhetoric, and there was more real change.

What made this green movement different? Part of the answer is a document called *Our Common Future*. It began as the report of the Brundtland Commission, which had been struck by the United Nations in 1983 to face the problem of " . . . the accelerating deterioration of the human environment and natural resources and the consequences of that deterioration for economic and social development." Presented to the General Assembly in 1987, it was built on a fascinating and pragmatic two-word concept: sustainable development. The formal definition of sustainable development was "development that meets the needs of the present without compromising the ability of future generations to meet their own needs." The genius of this can fly right past you if you don't read it carefully: You see, it's a détente. It doesn't say that the only way to save the world is to stop developing it. Instead, it's premised on the idea that development is inevitable, and that the way forward is to figure out how to do it so that we don't mortgage our future in the process. Before this, environmentalism was a political all-or-nothing standoff. After this, environmentalism started to become a matter of collective interest and focused on what we all had in common rather than on our conflicting agendas. Suddenly, nobody wanted to be left out. Environmentalism became an inclusive social force rather than a divisive political one, and that seemed to unlock things.

The memory of this hit me like a thunderbolt when I started thinking about a book on the future of brands and consumerism. Years ago, someone figured out a way that we could all be part of a green solution without having to hurl ourselves back to the Dark Ages, and that got people engaged. The key was finding common ground. So, does this same kind of common ground exist between we who consume and the corporations that profit from our appetites? Is there a perspective that could unlock our seemingly conflicting interests? Is there another way to look at consumerism that will allow we, the people, to direct its fate and make it more sustainable in *every* sense – economically, environmentally, socially?

I think there is – and as crazy as it may sound, I think the common ground is brands. Brands are the only thing that give ordinary people power over the behaviour of industry. Brands are a very big stick, and this big stick is almost entirely in our hands, not theirs. All we have to do is stop thinking like victims of marketing, and use it.

Consumer Republic is about why and how we possess this power, about how we can use it to shape change, and about the life we could have together as a result.

AFTER THE ORGY OF CONSUMPTION

(In which the food was terrible, and the portions were too small)

I have a dream. In this dream, I have purchased a toaster.

I'm quite excited about this toaster. It wasn't cheap, but then it is an Acme. Acme is a brand with real toaster cred. My new appliance is lovely to look at, built like a bank vault, and it apparently does a stellar job of browning bagels, which are my favourite breakfast food. I know this, because I have done my homework. Most of the people who have purchased the same brand of toaster are very pleased with this feature, and they've said so on the Google-powered brand-rating website that I always consult about such things. Let's call it *consumerrepublic.com*. I trust it because so many people contribute ratings to its brand trust indices, and because Google cleverly assigns authority to each rater and weights his or her opinions using one of its brilliant algorithm thingies. Thus, if this Internet resource tells me that Acme is a brilliant maker of toasters and that their products will reflect their owners' good taste and judgment, I'm inclined to believe it.

Except that mine is broken. Right out of the box. I'm a bit sad about this, because I'm not one to go out and buy a new toaster every five minutes. Or a new anything, for that matter. I, along with the rest of the world in my dream, prefer to buy things only when I need them, or when I'm genuinely inspired by them. I generally pay for them in cash, so that these things are really mine, rather than things I'm pretending are mine. That makes shopping for something like a toaster a bit of an event, and much more fun. It also means that I expect a lot when I plunk down my hard-earned money. When I bring a new purchase home to my modest, paid-for, tasteful residence, furnished only with objects that are useful and/or inspiring, I look forward to the unveiling. In this case, however, that shining moment, and the beginning of many years of mornings made sunnier by bagel perfection, must be postponed.

With a mildly exasperated sigh, I sit down at my computer. First, I go back to *consumerrepublic.com,* the brand-rating website that steered me to Acme, sign on, and add my purchase to the "pending resolution" file. On this imaginary website, every brand has one. It allows people in my situation to let the world know that there is a problem but that the jury is still out as to how that brand will deal with it. The site aggregates these complaints, and lists the information alongside its brand trust ratings. Brand marketers pay close attention to this leading indicator the way they used to watch the Dow, because this site doesn't just score brands for trust and performance – it also trends that score. When I looked at Acme's ratings while shopping for my dream toaster, I could see not only that they were pretty high but also that they had been gently trending higher for a long time. This company seemed not only to be good; it seemed to be getting better. Acme won't want to risk reversing that trend. Indeed, somewhere at Acme Global Headquarters, the potentially negative experience I'm having has already RSSed its way to a real-time customer satisfaction database. It may even have made a little *bong* noise when it got there. That would be cool. Regardless, Acme is already paying attention. Brand trust is too hard and expensive to earn to risk it on one broken toaster.

My next task is to contact Acme directly, which I do through their corporate website. Their site notices that I've come from *consumerrepublic.com*, so it jumps me up in the queue for a response. It doesn't take long, then, before Acme offers me two options on the spot. I can return the toaster for a replacement, or I can have it repaired. Being a guy who hates to see anything go to waste, I pick the second. In my dream, you can get things fixed. People are making their things last longer, and repair shops have made a big comeback. Noting my IP address, Acme geolocates me and is able to recommend a shop a few minutes away. The whole process so far has taken under ten minutes. I pack the toaster back into its reusable box and head for Main Street.

By the time I get to the shop, Acme has already sent an electronic docket to the repairperson. In this dream, he's a cranky but basically kind older fellow, a bit like Mr. Hooper on *Sesame Street*. The problem turns out to be simple to resolve. Mr. Hooper notices a screw that's loose and binding the mechanism. He fixes it on the spot, makes some trenchant remarks about the weather, and I'm on my way. Mr. Hooper closes the electronic docket, alerting Acme that the technical issue, at least, has been resolved. Acme, however, is not breathing easy just yet. In my dream world, their brand isn't off the hook until I say it is.

So, just to make them sweat, I take my time walking home. I wave as I pass all the other modest, tasteful, paid-for residences in my neighbourhood, stopping to talk to my next-door neighbour, who is enjoying the sunny morning by waxing his immaculately maintained ten-year-old car. It looks and runs like new, and people in the neighbourhood admire him for this. Finally home, I place the toaster on the kitchen counter and pop in a bagel. Moments later, golden brown perfection. Flushed with carbohydrate-induced bliss and feeling benevolent, I jump back on the web and remove my "pending resolution" flag at *consumerrepublic.com*. For good measure, I even head over to YouTube and tag Acme's latest commercial as "basically true" or "essentially credible." Something like that. A great rating from me on *consumerrepublic.com* will have to wait, though. It takes more than one perfect bagel to win me over.

So that's my dream. A world in which we live a little more simply, we buy things that are better rather than cheaper and more numerous, and we make them last. Where brands survive on selling better, fewer products, and fear letting us down more than they ever fear a decline in their stock price. And where the bagels are delicious.

That would *really* be cool.

———

I started work on *Consumer Republic* at what I hope will turn out to have been the lowest point in the history of consumerism. As I write, the civilized world is struggling to emerge from an economic near-disaster. This calamity's very roots, they tell us, lie in consumer debt and Wall Street's cynical exploitation of it. And this calamity has only momentarily distracted our attention from an even bigger mess, a planet in unprecedented distress from being plundered to meet the insatiable demands of its human inhabitants. More and more of us need and want more things, so we're ravaging the place like raccoons at a dumpster. More and more of us have been unwilling to wait until we can afford all that stuff, so we've mortgaged our futures like Wimpy hitting up Popeye for hamburger money. On CNN, serious-looking people in suits offer a glum play-by-play of the nasty comeuppance in financial markets, while a few channels up the dial at National Geographic, freaked-out-looking people in khaki shorts, predict the same for our environment. It's all a bit scary and, although nobody is putting it in exactly these words, it seems clear to me that the fundamental problem is too many people being sold too much stuff. Marketing, therefore, might essentially be at the bottom of all this.

It didn't take everybody else long to arrive at the same conclusion. A Harris Interactive poll from the spring of 2009, when things seemed economically at their worst, showed that two-thirds of Americans had already decided Madison Avenue was at least part of the problem. Half of those polled believed that most of the blame could be sent to that address.

It was a natural enough reaction. Marketing is an easy, logical scapegoat, if the problem is too much consumption. But, to me, this doesn't quite add up.

———

Most people understand that marketing has something to do with profitably meeting the demands of a group of people for a particular product or service. A marketer's job is to find a so-called "need," and then find a way to meet it and make some money in the process. To a marketer, consumer demand is assumed. It's like a natural resource to be exploited. It's just out there, like air. The marketer simply has to know how to recognize it, and then cater to it. However, if you think about it, there is a big, fat, and possibly baseless assumption behind that definition: that every sale of a product or service is self-validating. In other words, a marketer's responsibility ends when the money changes hands. If you bought it, it's because you needed it.

Yet if it's as simple as that, how can we explain this orgy of debt-fuelled consumption in the last decade or so? Surely these "needs" of ours haven't *increased* over time, have they? On the contrary, for a lot of us in the so-called developed world, they've diminished quite a bit. A couple of centuries ago, I could have presented a persuasive list of "needs" to anyone who cared to cater to them, from nutrition and personal hygiene to transportation and telecommunication. But now? I don't know about you, but I'm kind of running out of really pressing problems that could be solved with a trip to the mall. When fortunes can be made by combining tooth-whitening agents with mouthwash, or by devising a way for your car to recognize your mobile phone so that you can have conversations through the stereo, marketers have got to be scraping the bottom of the needs barrel.

To me, this is a paradox. If marketing is about needs, and we need less today than we ever have, why is there more marketing? More perplexing still, why does it seem to be working? Working so well, in fact, that it risks destroying our way of life? Either marketing never was about needs in the first place, or none of us understood what a need really was.

Well, almost none of us. Most people with a passing interest in psychology have at some point run into the work of Abraham Maslow. His Hierarchy of Needs is a staple theory of the science, and it's been sticky and viral because of its intuitive and simple logic: We humans will focus our attention on meeting needs in a predictable sequence, and that sequence will put matters of survival first and self-actualization last. In other words, nobody is going to give much thought to his personal value system or his inner child if he's hungry and cold. Conversely, if a person is relatively safe, warm, and well fed, and enjoys the support of a social system, she will have time to spend on the bigger questions of morality and her purpose in the world. These then become her "needs." This logic presents two interesting implications for what marketing really is: First, it says that our definition of "needs" is fluid and contextual. Second, it says that what motivates the way we meet our needs evolves inevitably from being a matter of survival – *I'm hungry* – to something more to do with self-expression – *This is who I am.*

Maslow proposed his hierarchy as a way of explaining individual human behaviour. But can it explain the behaviour of societies, too? Do we collectively move in a way that mirrors our individual behaviours? I think, more often than not, we do. When you look at our collective hierarchy of needs, it would be hard to dispute that, as a group, we've worked our way considerably up the ladder over the past century, and that many of us are fortunate enough to have our basic needs consistently met. When an entire community has its basic needs met, it will inevitably tend to turn its attention to values, and to the pursuit of self-esteem, achievement, and enlightenment. Without fear, societies evolve more freely. It's our collective aspiration. As if to underscore the point, it seems like only yesterday that the United States inaugurated a president whose election campaign made a point of speaking more loudly to our better selves than it did to our fear of real or imagined threats to our survival. Based on the world's reaction back on that giddy November 4, 2008, election night, humanity seemed ready to ascend, ready to dedicate ourselves to being *better* rather than just being *safe*. Collective self-actualization was nigh. We were buying it big time.

Yet a little more than three weeks after that night, on November 29, 2008 – Black Friday, so named because it's the time of year when American retailers are said to cross the line between losing and making money, and the official start of the holiday shopping season – a temporary worker at the Walmart at Green Acres Mall in Valley Stream, New York, was trampled to death by a mob of shoppers. They had been gathering in front of the store since the previous day, champing at the bit to take advantage of bargains. The local police had deployed crowd control officers as early as 3:30 a.m., and by 5:00 a.m., according to a *New York Times* reporter, "The crowd of more than 2,000 had become a rabble and could be held back no longer." A rabble? At Walmart? It was an unusually dramatic expression of the mania of consumerism, with a tragic and thankfully rare result. But its symbolic power is undeniable: Here, on the pivotal day of the year when retailers were finally moving into the black, they seemed to be depending on humanity's worst urges to do it. The scene, according to an investigating police officer, was "utter chaos," and the crowd "out of control." And the lure was not sustenance or shelter or escape from predators, but video games, paper towels, power tools, and fleece wear. We were still buying those, too.

Again, this just doesn't make sense. Something is broken, here. On the one hand, we have those opportunistic marketers: Believing that their role in the world is to relieve us of our money by meeting our "needs," they sell us everything as though our lives depended on buying it. Their default tool is urgency. Urgency to whiten and deodorize, to seem more prosperous than our neighbours, to pay less than those same neighbours in the process, to act now before it's all gone. High-definition televisions are being brought to market as urgently as if they were bags of rice thrown to the starving from the backs of Red Cross trucks. On the other hand, scrambling after them are we, the consumers. Made fools of once too often, egged on by pundits, too vain to acknowledge our own vanity, we behave as if consumption were a competitive sport in which whoever gets the most for the least wins. Which is surely not the path to self-actualization, or any other legitimate need for that matter. We and the marketers who sell to us have locked ourselves into a kind of destructive codependency. Is it any wonder we're all in debt? Is it any wonder that vast economies are erupting in far-flung corners of the planet premised solely on the making of more things for less money? Is it any wonder that the planet is groaning under the strain?

No, it is not. What's amazing, in fact, is that things aren't worse than they are.

I don't think I'm alone in observing this, either. I think people are beginning to feel a sense of culpability. I've lived through a few Main Street recessions, but never one that raised the questions that this one has about the morality of consuming: about how much is enough; about the social meaning of material things, or whether the things we buy should have any social meaning at all; about personal accountability. We aren't necessarily saying so out loud, but we know we had a hand in this.

Still, if history teaches us nothing else, it certainly teaches us that humans won't bear the weight of repentance for long. We don't like hair shirts, even if they are on sale. We are built to be hopeful. So, in the next short while, two things will inevitably happen. First, people will look for someone that history can blame for this so they can get on with their lives. And second, people will return to some modified version of their natural state, which, here in the "developed world," means consuming. What worries me is, we really will blame branded marketing. When the dust has settled and everyone feels we've flagellated ourselves enough, we're going to decide once and for all that corporations and their evil organ grinder's monkeys, brands, have been the problem.

But before we toss the bathwater of marketing out the window, let's make sure we see the brand baby for what it is, and for what it could be. So what is it?

Imagine that you have a headache.

Unable to stand it any more, you make for the nearest drug store and face the shelf where they keep the pain relievers. If you are like roughly a third of North Americans, you will reach for Tylenol. Why? Right next to it, there is a generic product that is identical — I mean *identical* — in its formulation. It contains 325 mg of acetaminophen per tablet, just like regular Tylenol. It is dollars cheaper, pharmacologically the same, and, by statute, therapeutically equivalent. Why on earth are you paying more? Are you a fool?

No, you are not. Whether or not you're willing to admit it, that extra couple of dollars is buying you two kinds of insurance: One, that you can delegate to Johnson & Johnson the task of solving your headache rather than having to learn the pharmacology of acetaminophen for yourself. And, two, that if something goes wrong, someone will take responsibility.

One day, in 1982, something did go wrong. A murderer tampered with Tylenol on the shelves of a Chicago drug store, and killed seven people. Johnson & Johnson's response became a case study in public relations. From their unprecedented transparency with the press, to their willingness to destroy millions of dollars' worth of product as a precaution, to their rapid and brilliant innovation of security features, they did everything right and quickly. Their market share fell to 7 per cent from 37 per cent in the immediate aftermath of the tragedy, but it rebounded to 30 per cent within twelve months of the incident. They remain today the most trusted analgesic brand in the market.

When this happened, the corporation that makes Tylenol did more than they had to do. Even allowing for some margin of human decency, there is an important practical reason why Johnson & Johnson took responsibility so completely and so vigorously: their brand. The fame of the Tylenol name made their response to the crisis public. Consumers became a jury, and this was Tylenol's trial of a lifetime.

That's why we pay more than we need to for a lot of the products we buy. That's why brands matter to us, however secretly or unconsciously. Because they make corporations accountable, and in doing that they give us power.

In *Consumer Republic*, I want to do three things:

First, I want to convince you that you have this power. I'm going to give you a glimpse behind the curtain of marketing and show you the role that we as consumers really play in that process.

Then, I'm going to offer a different, more contemporary, and relevant way to look at the role that brands and consumption play in our lives. I want to convince you that we need to bury the idea of status, right now, and that something much healthier and more interesting is already starting to replace it. In doing this, I hope to convince you that making brands work for us is much more satisfying and productive than pretending they don't matter.

Finally, I want to get you excited about why this is our

moment. We're warned constantly that we should expect less from the future than we became accustomed to in the past. I think that means we should also expect *better*, and I think we finally have in our hands the means to say so and the power to back it up. Commerce has come a long way from the time when the only indication of the health of a marketer's business was whether the merchandise was moving or not. Now, they can see and hear trouble coming before it gets there. Now, as never before, marketers can be influenced to do what we want them to do, as a condition of remaining in business.

Consumer Republic isn't about guilt and doom. It's about possibility. This moment in our history, with its crisis and its empowering social and technological changes, has finally given consumers the genuine autonomy we were meant to have all along. This book is about what to do with it.

PART ONE

THE CORPORATION IS A COW

A BRIEF CULTURAL HISTORY OF BRANDS,

STARRING YOU

"The consumer is not a moron. She's your wife."

The words are famously those of the late David Ogilvy, a titan of advertising's golden age in the 1960s, and by all reports a lovely gentleman who spent his waning years in a castle in the south of France. Our parents and grandparents bought this castle for him with every Hathaway shirt, bottle of Schweppes soda, and bar of Dove soap they purchased in response to his agency's clever advertising in the 1960s and 1970s. For many, many years, the phrase was routinely quoted by ad people – out of its original context, which I'll come back to in a moment – as an admonition to be respectful of consumers in their work. Having laboured in that vineyard for so long, two things have always struck me about this dictum. The first, of course, is that it's remarkable he felt such an admonition was necessary at all – the ad biz's reputation for cynicism is not wholly unearned, I'm afraid. The second is more interesting: Ogilvy's statement was actually a tacit admission that consumers are wily prey (the rest of the quote is, "Do not insult her intelligence"). He may as well have said, "You can't make people part with their money by underestimating them."

Brands, to Ogilvy, were the hunters, and advertising was the weapon, and he worried that this weapon, if misused, would lose its power and the hunters would go hungry. To people in advertising, the distinction is essential. It reminds them that bad advertising can kill a brand, and that this would be an incalculable loss. Ads come and go like the weather, but a brand is priceless and takes a long time and a lot of money to build. The minute it loses its value to the consumer, it loses its value to the corporation behind it.

In other words, even from the earliest days of branded marketing, consumers were never really prey at all. We've always been worthy adversaries, and every bit as much hunters as the marketers are.

CHAPTER ONE

PRO LOGO

Some years back, I was the Advertising Manager at Panasonic. Panasonic was and is a brand belonging to a vast Japanese electronics enterprise called Matsushita. This manufacturing giant had always had a complicated relationship with the whole idea of branding because, like many industrial giants, and especially those in Japan at that time, they fundamentally believed that the key to sustainable profitability was volume. They mostly preferred to make a small profit margin on each one of a great many copies of a product rather than to make a large margin on each one of a few. Their whole system of production was aimed at this objective, because they knew that more volume promoted more efficiency, and more efficiency produced greater profits. This notion was deeply embedded in the company's culture, as it was in many Japanese companies then, thanks partly to a sort of genesis myth involving its founder. Konosuke Matsushita, inspired by the communal water well in the prefecture where he grew up, believed in the power and justice of abundance, and he saw creating abundance as his purpose in life.

In their pursuit of all that volume, the factories that produced items like VCRs would contract their capacity to other brands besides their own. It was whispered at the time that more than a dozen different brands of VCR rolled off Matsushita's assembly lines, many of those direct competitors to Panasonic. From the perspective of the factory bosses, that was good. It meant more production, more efficiency, more profit, and cheaper products for you and me. But from the perspective of their sales operations worldwide, it was a little bit vexing, and you can guess why: If people could buy a "Panasonic" VCR from any one of a dozen brands, how could that not diminish the value of buying one from Panasonic? How could that not drive prices down and turn the technology into a commodity? Certainly, nobody who sold Panasonic VCRs was telling customers that they could get the same thing elsewhere, and possibly for less. But you can be sure that lots of "elsewhere" salespeople were sharing the information freely. It drove their dealers mad. And before too many years had gone by, large tracts of the consuming public had VCRs in their living rooms that shared two characteristics: the clock was flashing 12:00, and the machine was probably made by the people who make Panasonics.

You can see where this is going. VCR dealers were clamouring for lower wholesale pricing, because the product was becoming a commodity, while the factory bosses in Japan were reaching the conclusion that branding didn't matter very much at all. Marketing spending was gradually choked off, every imaginable cost was driven out of the system, and the product became cheaper every year instead of better (an important theme I'll return to later in the book). The "abundance" assumption was slowly backfiring on Matsushita, a fate averted only by the innovation of a replacement technology, the DVD player.

In the middle of all this, an interesting debate took place at the office where I worked. Into the company's lap fell a provocative snippet of market intelligence published by a trade journal. It was the result of a simple experiment conducted by the Dutch electronics company Philips. Philips was a great innovator at the time, having given us, among other things, the Compact Cassette and the CD. But innovation is expensive and risky. As a lot of consumer electronics products found themselves under the threat of commoditization (see "volume = profit" above), Philips might have legitimately worried whether innovation could ever consistently pay out for them. In a world of functionally similar little black-and-silver boxes, what was their brand actually worth? And so they set out to find the answer empirically.

The experiment went like this: Two groups of consumers in the Netherlands were each shown a television set, along with a list of specifications for that set. The TVs were identical in every way, both in appearance and in their specifications. They looked the same, worked the same way, had the same picture and sound quality, and so on. There was really only one difference. One set bore the Philips brand name on the front of its cabinet, and the other bore no brand name at all. The researchers' essential question to the study's participants was simply, "How much would you pay for this television set?" The answer will probably not surprise you. The people who were evaluating the branded TV were willing to pay more for it, something on the order of 20 per cent more than they'd pay for the generic set. For some reason, to these hunting consumers, the branded television looked like tastier quarry. Why?

There are three possible answers to this question. The first is the answer marketers might glibly give: consumers trust the branded product more than the unbranded one. The second is the answer a lot of consumers might give if they were asked in a study like this: they'd pay more for the branded product because they think it's going to be better. The third possible answer is the right one: Consumers would pay more for the branded television set because that premium buys them some insurance. Having Philips put their name on the box makes them responsible for it, just as giving the chemical acetaminophen the brand name Tylenol does. Yes, the likelihood is that this television will be better, because Philips' observable prosperity suggests that they get this stuff right more often than they get it wrong. But more than this, their name gives customers someone to blame and somewhere to go if the product disappoints them (or worse, as in the Tylenol case). For the people in the study, that insurance was easily worth a 20 per cent premium. They weren't fools – they just had better things to do than become television experts as a precondition for buying one. They knew that if a big company was willing to put their famous name on a product, buying their product wouldn't be as risky as purchasing one whose maker preferred that its provenance remain a mystery. In other words, these people weren't only expecting to pay for what was in the box. They were also expecting – and willing – to pay for who put it there.

The discussion around the cafeteria table at Panasonic was, not surprisingly, lively, given the company's rather staid corporate culture and its production-focused business model. Some thought that this was interesting proof that investing in the Panasonic brand was a good idea, yes, even if it ended up adding to the cost of marketing a VCR. Others believed – and it just sounds so darned sensible when you put it this way – that all consumers really want is the best possible product. Certainly, that was the view of the factory bosses in Japan. They figured that if they just made the best TVs and VCRs they could at the lowest possible prices, everybody would be happy. And there ended the debate. Within a few years, VCRs had become so inexpensive and so unprofitable for retailers that only big box stores could really afford to sell them. Less and less production was done in Japan, and these things became all but disposable. But for its well-timed obsolescence, it's tough to imagine where the VCR business would have gone from there, or how any-body's life would have been better for it.

So what *are* we hunting for? As consumers, do we really just want the best product at the lowest price? You're probably nodding, but I don't think it's that simple. I think you might be kidding yourself. I think those Dutch people Philips used as mar-keting guinea pigs pointed the way to a bigger truth, the truth that stupid marketing and misguided social pressure keep us from facing whenever we reach for our wallets: brands are useful to us because they shift accountability away from the buyer and on to the seller. Which is right where we want it, thank you very much. I don't know about you, but I have enough to worry about without having to look warily over my shoulder at every appliance in my house as if it were silently plotting against me. That flashing 12:00 was bad enough.

———

For a taste of a world without brands, take a taxi.

In New York City, all the taxis are yellow. The legal ones, anyway. They're all painted exactly the same shade (Dupont M6284 or the equivalent), and wear the same strange little logo and the same medallion signifying their legitimacy in the eyes of the all-powerful Taxi and Limousine Commission. They all charge the same price, all have Plexiglas shields between the driver and the passengers, all have the same video display in the back seat incessantly blaring weather reports, and all have the same list of rules posted where you can see them as you bump and lurch your way around the boroughs. No sane person in New York City is picky about which cab they get into as long as it conforms to this description. They take the first one that will stop for them, discriminating possibly only on the basis of the direction in which it's pointed. Taxis are all pretty much as good as they need to be in order to conform to the law, and pretty much no better than that. They're all essentially the same. There isn't what you and I would call "choice."

What does that get us? Well, largely because of the iron fist of regulation, it gets us a reliable and effective accessory to New York City's public transit system. So that's good. What it doesn't get us is motivated service delivery or an urge to excel at satisfying customers. Even tipping can't really be said to encourage extraordinary service – it's unlikely you'll ever ride with the same driver again or that he'd remember you. The drivers of these vehicles depend on aggression and alertness to make their money, that and a reasonable command of the city's geography. To them, passengers are prey, and the cabbie who gets to them first and is quickest to screech to a halt in front of them gets to eat. The owners of the cabs, meanwhile, are utterly invisible to us. If we look, we can see their names posted in the cabs, but they're never names we recognize. Most certainly, they're never names we can store away in our minds for future reference or retribution. But for the bureaucratic conscience of the ironically acronymed TLC, we are utterly powerless in this transaction. And that's what happens when you remove choice from a marketplace. Everything is no better than it absolutely has to be, and we need the government to protect us from getting taken for a ride other than the one we'd planned on.

Choice is the very centre of our power as consumers. As long as we have options, the people who are trying to sell us things have to try that much harder to get our business. They have to try to make a better and more attractive product, they have to try to make that product as relevant to us as they can, and they have to try to stay pleasantly in our faces before, during, and after the purchase so that we like and trust them. This trying harder usually produces all sorts of benefits in terms of competitiveness and efficiency in our economy, and collaterally maybe even in our society. The fact of choice enables the free market, and makes it accountable. Moreover, choice counterbalances what would otherwise be an irresistible temptation for corporations to see how little they can get away with giving us in exchange for our money. Make no mistake, that urge is still an engine of marketing – it's the ugly cousin of "efficiency" – but it gets blunted by the constant awareness that you and I can always take our money elsewhere. Marketers have to make their products distinctive, and they have to offer some kind of special value. So crucial is this idea to protecting us and our system of commerce that many countries have laws to prevent corporations from being in cahoots on things like pricing in order to preserve choice. Choices give us power, and brands are what those choices are called. You can't have one without the other.

But that truth only makes the case for accepting that brands are a necessary fact of life. What if I told you that the usefulness of brands doesn't stop at the cash register? What if I told you that a brand can keep working for you long after you've parted with your money? Would you believe me? Or, more to the point, would you be willing to admit it?

Let's settle it over a drink.

———

Of all the branded products that corporations try to sell us, one of the most fascinating is beer. Intrinsically, this product has all the marketing potential of gravel. Most beers are made with the same four ingredients: water, hops, malt, and yeast. The recipe is thought to be well over ten thousand years old. It's so easy to make that people do it in their basements. Beer is the most widely consumed alcoholic beverage in the world, and ranks behind only water and tea as the most widely consumed beverage, period. By any rational measure, this stuff ought to be flowing from our kitchen taps. If you were from another planet, you might conclude that beer is essential to life and no more requires or responds to branded marketing than does air, water, or the urge to reproduce.

And yet it does. Despite its long history, despite its ubiquity, despite the monotony of its recipe, few products attract more sheer marketing energy. Beer is a business worth something like $300 billion a year globally, and the number of brand names corporations have given to the amber nectar is surely in the thousands. They wouldn't do it if it didn't work. So why does it?

The best way to begin to understand the answer is to step back and look more broadly at the way we choose beverages. Most of us don't have one favourite thing to drink. We probably enjoy a few kinds of juices, maybe milk, a handful of soft drinks, perhaps one or more kinds of alcoholic beverages, coffee and tea, and of course water. A "drink" is not a commodity to

most of us. We have a menu in our heads, and we choose something from it every time we pause for a sip, nip, or gulp.
Naturally, that choice is going to be a little bit functional. We
might be hot and thirsty, or chilled and in need of warming up,
or stressed and in need of relaxation. However, most of the time
there is a great deal more to it than that.

A soft drink company I worked with explained it this way.
After you get past availability and physical needs, three things
guide the choice of a beverage: whom we're with, the mood
we're in, and the emotional atmosphere we're trying to achieve.
To understand where their product fits into their customers'
lives, they visualized a three-dimensional universe, with those
three things as its dimensions. The choice of any drink, they
believed, depended upon the occasion in which we were drinking it. Whiskey, for example, would suit a more intimate setting,
a more sober mood, and a more reflective state of mind. Colas
might suit a more social situation, a more cheerful mood, and
a more child-like emotional state. Champagne, green tea, hot
cocoa, and sports drinks all had their own prototypical situations. Why "prototypical"? Obviously, people can and do drink
whatever they want whenever they want. But, aside from its
intrinsic charms, every beverage turns out to have its own social
meaning, and that's the key. Contrary to popular opinion, it's
when and not *who* that is most often the foundation of "target-
ing" in the beverage market.

Fine for marketers, but what possible use is all this to us as
consumers? Let's look at it from the vantage point of our bar
stool:

Let's say you and I are going to meet for that drink. We
don't know each other that well but you've agreed to meet me
after work. We arrive at the same time, we sit at the bar, and

the bartender comes over and takes our order. Let's say mine is bourbon, straight up. Okay, quick: What goes through your mind? Are you wondering if I'm a dissipated writer with a drinking problem? Or maybe have some kind of unresolved macho issue? What does this suggest about the kind of evening we're going to have? Now, what if I order a Cosmopolitan instead? Now what do you think? What if it were Chardonnay? Diet Coke? Soda with lime? Absinthe? If you're like most people, you are able to instantly conjure up a tidy set of expectations about me and the hours ahead, just based on that moment. And what if I had ordered beer? Well, those guys at the soft drink company would say that beer is a very social beverage, most at home in cheerful situations, and informal and regressive in its character. My ordering a beer would have communicated the same message as my showing up to meet you wearing Levi's: I'm going to be at ease in your company.

In other words, our choice of beverage isn't just a way to satisfy ourselves. It is also frequently a form of communication, a social signal, one that we often deploy unconsciously, and most certainly from time to time very consciously. Think about the drink order you might make on a first date with someone who is a little out of your league and how carefully you might consider that decision. If, for example, I were an opera-singing supermodel Olympian and card-carrying MENSA member, you probably wouldn't begin our evening by ordering a Jack Daniel's and a Budweiser chaser.

If the foregoing seems preposterous, consider this case in point: When President Barack Obama decided to try to broker peace in a very tense and public conflict between a black Harvard professor and a white cop who arrested the professor in his own home in Cambridge, Massachusetts, he used the symbolic power of the beer occasion to set the tone. Describing it as "three folks having a drink at the end of the day," he held the meeting at a picnic table and beer is what he served. The press dubbed it "The Beer Summit," and in the pre-meeting roundtable, what was the first question asked by a reporter? "What beer will President Obama serve his guests?" This "social signal" power of choice-making, you see, doesn't stop at the category of beverage you choose. Even within a single category of beverage, each brand has its own meaning and sends its own signals. Ordering a Bud sends a different signal than ordering a Stella Artois, or a Guinness, or a Lone Star. The same holds true for many of the products we wear, drive, eat, read, play with, watch, and listen to. If you still doubt that brands are a social code, ask a rapper. Or a screenplay writer. Or the President.

So how should consumers feel about that?

The countless strangers I've watched through the one-way glass in focus groups over the years claim to think it's corporate manipulation, and they vehemently deny being influenced by it. With few if any exceptions, people are repulsed by the idea that "image" affects their purchase decisions. In many product categories, it's the very epicentre of the war consumers see themselves as having with the marketers who are trying to take their money. I'm not unsympathetic. Sometimes, invented social signals really are just lame attempts at manipulation (I can't believe anybody seriously thinks they can convince me that the right body spray will make me irresistible to supermodels in an elevator). And there probably is some social value in *not* shouting out the fact that our brand choices send social signals. Those signals would somehow have less authenticity and, therefore, less power if we were all publicly self-conscious about them. But we're not victims in the image game. Far from it.

For one thing, constructing an image for yourself is an entertaining exercise in self-expression. Yes, like most forms of entertainment, there are some cringingly cautionary stories of what happens when people go too far or take it too seriously. But for a well-adjusted, ordinary person, it can be amusing to specify the kind of gin you want in your martini the way James Bond does, or to wear the same brand of sunglasses as Lance Armstrong, or to declare your allegiance in the great cola schism. As long as it's your choice and exercised authentically and with moderation, it's harmless, amusing pop culture sport at the very least. It's less geeky than Six Degrees of Kevin Bacon, and the language of brands is so universal that everyone can play.

At best, it's much more than that. The assertion of individuality through observable consumption has been a feature of prosperous, free societies since consumerism began (though rarely without some ambivalence, it's fair to add). It was, in fact, its original motivating force. Historian Peter Stearns, writing on the history of consumerism as a cultural force in history, acknowledged that, along with its dangers, "[consumerism] often stands for freedom and individual choice. This was true in the past and remains true for many today. It often stands as well for an attack on rigid social order or gender hierarchy." This is so profoundly true, in fact, that totalitarianism of every sort, from Nazism to Soviet Communism and even to certain fundamentalist religious movements, almost always features an anti-consumerist theme. If you want to subjugate a people, start by forbidding them to shop. Consumerism subverts any social agenda that features stern homogeneity as an objective, and totalitarianisms don't like that, whereas almost any expression of personal autonomy, so long as it doesn't harm others, is a sign of a healthy society. Much as it might make us squirm to think so, that expression includes consumerism.

A second, maybe more immediately powerful reason why the social meaning of brands is too important to dismiss is its ability to keep companies scared straight. The companies whose brands depend on pop culture legitimacy to stay alive know two things that keep them up at night. They know that they are not fully in control of social meaning: that meaning is at least partly given to brands by us. And they know that if something goes wrong, it's going to be very hard to fix. Consumers will forgive the odd failed product, but if something goes wrong with the social meaning of a brand, it enters the vernacular, and the effects can linger for a very long time. "Edsel" remains slang for a marketing failure more than half a century after the Ford Motor Company ceased production of the product. Levi Strauss's Dockers brand spent years in the fashion wilderness before it could shake its association with nerds and men who didn't know how to deal with Casual Fridays. When ignominy gets a name, it sticks.

Here's a famous case that illustrates just how important social meaning is, and how much corporations dread it going wrong:

In 2000, when Naomi Klein decided to out globalization and bad corporate behaviour in her blockbuster *No Logo*, she cleverly chose to make brands the poster child for evil. She clearly understood that corporate malfeasance and the way companies make the products we buy were going to be abstractions for most of her readers, inducing in us the same helpless detachment we feel towards all forms of tyranny in faraway places. So she gave globalization a name we could all understand: branding. By linking her polemic to what we brought home from the mall last Saturday, she made her stories personal, accessible, and painful for us. It was a brilliant rhetorical ploy. And nobody got it worse than Nike. The brand turns up no fewer than thirty-seven times in *No Logo*, and it's not a flattering picture.

Why did Klein pick Nike? There were surely many other targets among athletic footwear brands. Why not take aim at the entire running shoe business? Yet Adidas turns up in the index only five times, Reebok six, Converse – makers of the ubiquitous and cheap-chic Chuck Taylors, and since purchased by Nike – not once. So why Nike? The answer is glaringly obvious: As a brand, Nike was at the top of its game in the late '90s. Not only was the company successful globally, but it had also managed to get its brand adopted by an astoundingly diverse array of pop culture tribes. The brand meant something to sports heroes, weekend warriors, thugs and couch potatoes alike, in all walks of life, in just about every country in the world. Nike had risen above specialization, above "target market," above the dreary details of product functionality. By the mid-1990s, when Klein picked up the story, Nike wasn't a product any more. It was a statement. If she could change the meaning of that statement, she could do more harm to her enemy, more quickly and on a larger scale than all the reasoned academic argument in the universe.

Brands were not behind the crimes described in *No Logo*, but they did make those crimes more interesting. Nike was the best target simply because it had the most valuable high-profile brand in the sneaker business. Focusing on it was the way to make the greatest number of people squirm, and it got our attention.

It got Nike's attention, too. The public flaying of their brand was a game-changer for the running shoe company. There is very little on the public record to show that Nike made any connection between good behaviour and good branding in the late 1990s; their marketing legacy suggests they were much more preoccupied with protecting their brand's street cred. But read their annual report or visit their website today, and one is left with the impression that the corporation is as preoccupied with social responsibility as it is with sports. Page after page on their corporate site deals with the environment, workers and factories, procurement and vendor certification, governance, charitable spending, and building links between sustainability and innovation, from the Amazon rain forest to inner city streets. In the corporate vernacular, it's very "proactive" about its citizenship. What's more, none of it is written in the cloyingly formal, spinny language that blights the About Us pages of most corporate sites. It's branded like crazy, which is exactly the point. Nike is a $19 billion empire built on social meaning, existing because millions of people decided its brand was cool. It wasn't the accusations of a twenty-nine-year-old Canadian journalist and former "mall rat" that made Nike especially uncomfortable, it was the specific asset that those words threatened to devalue: the social meaning of their brand.

In 1995, I paid a visit to Dan Wieden, co-founder of Wieden+Kennedy, Nike's ad agency since the 1980s. Wieden is famously close to Nike boss Phil Knight, and could fairly be described, gender notwithstanding, as the brand's true muse. In our conversation, I asked him what the Nike brand's superpower really was, where the magic "cred" came from. His pugnacious reply: "Authenticity." That's what was at stake when Naomi Klein called Nike a "brand bully." You can't sell personal empowerment if people think you're a bully. Without that authenticity, it wouldn't matter how brilliantly designed, well made, or cheap Nike products were. They'd never sell another shoe. And that – whether you personally choose to play the image game or not – is the real reason that we aren't victims of it. We're anything but. Nike went to a lot of trouble to be seen to clean up its act, so much so that by one assessment they are today ranked among the world's most ethical corporations. They did that because they were afraid of what we would think of them, and eventually of each other, for buying their stuff.

Putting the social meaning gun to the head of Nike's brand was transformational. That is serious leverage, and it proves once again the power of brands in the hands of consumers. Which raises the question: Why on earth, Naomi, would you want to live in a world with no logos?

———

Do you remember the ritual of bringing home your report card from school? Maybe you handed your mom the envelope and all you had to do was stand there waiting for praise to cascade down upon you. But if you were like me, every once in a while you shuffled home from school like a dead man walking, gave Mom the envelope with downcast eyes, and waited, flinching, for the heavy sigh when she read Mr. Quigley's comments about how utterly giftless you were at calculus.

The analogous moment in the world of branded marketing is the time spent scrutinizing tracking study reports. A tracking study is a comprehensive survey that's repeated, almost like a political poll, at regular intervals so that a corporation can monitor trends in how people are feeling about them and what they sell. By asking the same questions to the same kinds of people repeatedly over time, a company can get a sense of which way the wind is blowing, image-wise, of how effective their recent marketing has been, and of any trouble ahead. Tracking-type market research is used for all kinds of things, from monitoring price sensitivity to customer service satisfaction, but what seems to be the most common use, and the one that is likely to fill the room with the most senior executives on report card day, is brand tracking.

What are all those anxious suits there to hear? They are there to hear how many people have heard of their brand, how many of them are familiar with it, and what those people think of it. Yes, typically, a study like this will ask some questions about satisfaction with a company's product and perceptions of its competitors (all misery being derived, of course, from comparison, and misery being the true purpose of market research). However, the meat of a typical tracking study report, the part that will make brand managers lean forward at the table and their bosses switch off their BlackBerrys, is the part where the smug, nerdy research consultant tells them what consumers think of the name they put on the stuff they sell. The name they count on to make those products more attractive, to justify their pricing, to support their stock price, and to allow them to hold their heads high at cocktail parties when people ask them where they work. If the news is good, the meeting will be short and pleasant. If it's bad, it will be tense, long, and sometimes personal. Enough of those, and people lose their jobs.

A lot has changed for marketing since the days of the VCR, and what I think has changed the most is marketers' attitudes toward their brands. Consumer electronics corporations, in particular, went nuts in those days trying to emulate the Japanese industrial formula of profit through volume. They took field trips to Japan to study the miracle of making more money by making more stuff. Industry became obsessed with manufacturing techniques and believed that their efficiently produced, mostly flawless products would just sell themselves (the same delusion that afflicts many of today's web entrepreneurs). But most marketers seem to have learned since those years that a single-minded focus on what a product does, how it works, and how to make it ends up producing an unprofitable commodity. That fate is especially likely if, as is often the case today, they don't even own the factories where their products are made. Endorsement and accountability, on the other hand, are claims that a company can make and defend regardless of the mechanics of production, and these are exactly the attributes a brand is supposed to declare. For many marketers, that brand is really all they've got, their only asset, the only thing they can't rent. There is no secret sauce, no ironclad patent, no proprietary process that ensures sustainable desirability. When a company doesn't even own its own factories, the name on its product becomes life and death for that corporation. Brands become religion.

But feedback from the marketplace isn't just about keeping score. Much more than this, it's a measure of our receptiveness to a label; of how likely we are to respond positively to the *next* thing they try to sell. So, just as Mr. Quigley's black-hearted opprobrium of your calculus skills would predict how pleasant the dinner table was going to be on report card night, so brand tracking, for a marketer, predicts what business is going to be like in the fiscal quarters ahead. The marketer knows that today's disillusioned consumer is tomorrow's lost business. Those losses will hit the business twice: once in sales it doesn't make, and a second time when it eventually has to buy back that goodwill with marketing dollars. That's why how much regard we have for a brand, from ketchup to cars, gets corporate attention.

A brand opens a channel between the corporate world and our kitchens, living rooms, closets, and garages. We should care about brands because they shift accountability to sellers, they create the choice that keeps consumers in control of marketplaces, and they can acquire useful social meaning. But of all the reasons we should give a fig about the labels on the products we buy, that's the big one. Brands make corporations listen.

Now, let's have a look at what they hear.

CHAPTER TWO

THE CORPORATION IS A COW

I t took about forty years to kill advertising. You may not
have realized it was dead, but it is.

The fatal wound was administered in 1957 by Vance
Packard with his million-seller exposé *The Hidden Persuaders*.
The subtitle describes the bullet fairly accurately: *What makes
us buy, believe – and even vote – the way we do. An introduction to the new world of symbol manipulation and motivational
research.* In the collective consciousness of popular culture,
Packard outed marketing as a business of shrewd deceptions and
cynical ruses (possibly in the process giving the manipulation
business more credit than it was due). From that moment
onward, it was assumed that we should doubt anything brands
told us.

After *The Hidden Persuaders*, advertising thrashed about
and gradually bled to death until its final gasp, around the time
of *The Simpsons* episode "The Itchy & Scratchy & Poochie
Show," which aired in February 1997. Before Vance Packard, it
was supposedly possible to believe that corporations messed
with our psyches without our being aware of it, and used this

35

power to force us into buying things we didn't want. After Itchy, Scratchy, and Poochie (with Lisa's devastating send-up of focus group research: "Why is that mirror sneezing?"), there simply could not have been anyone left within reach of a television who still thought that ads, or any kind of branded marketing, possessed ineffable power over our minds. The jig was up. We were on to their game. Advertising, by definition, would forever more be due the same sort of scorn and skepticism as cats have for leashes.

Nothing stands in the way of enlightened consumerism more stubbornly than the belief that we are victims of marketing. Or, that other people are. (I've never actually met anyone who thought that they, themselves, were blinded by its mesmerizing charms.) Yet, with the promotional support of well-meaning academics and journalists, the cultural artifact of corporate manipulation through the media has sustained itself long after things stopped being quite so black and white. It may be true that marketing was once a chillingly empirical process in which corporations experimented with various kinds of cheese to see which one would attract us mice in the greatest numbers. Now it's more often true that those same marketers are asking us mice to help them design the traps. Most brands today rely on our permission to exist, let alone to mean anything. Mighty corporations, standing astride mountains of money, find themselves nervously looking in our direction as if they were teens at a prom hoping to be asked to dance. If this picture is a surprising one to you, that's only because it's new. The final subversion of old-school corporate brand marketing happened quietly but certainly in the 1990s, recently enough that most of us were there to see it and, without realizing it, even help it along.

There are plenty of theories about what made the '90s what

they were. Some are based on the influence of the disaffected Generation X, who came bitterly of age in the shadow of affluent, self-mythologizing Baby Boomers. Others are formulated on the premise that a devastating recession threatened at the time to reset the idea of wealth and aspiration forever; still others, on the fact that technology and an explosion of new media options began to place more cultural control in the hands of the people. All played a role in a pretty powerful equation: cynical generation + interrupted materialism + rapid, empowering change = no orthodoxy is safe. Not even the orthodoxy of brands. One minute, our TVs were tuned into the shiny, perfect bourgeois dream worlds of *L.A. Law* and *The Cosby Show* in the sunshine of Reagan's America, and the next minute into the grit and moral murk of *NYPD Blue* and the nihilistic mockfest of *Seinfeld*. In almost no time at all, we went from being dreamers and idealists about our lifestyles to being unwilling to confess that we even had one. If one were in the business of selling dreams, as the ad biz had been in its heyday, you can see how all this might be a problem.

The central theme in all of this social change was blunt rejection. I don't mean the hippie counterculture variety, where people rejected a status quo because they thought they could do better. I mean the "What's the point?" kind of rejection. It was as if popular culture had lost its job and was now spending its days on the couch, unshaven, in its bathrobe, eating pork rinds and making fun of Jerry Springer's guests. In all forms of popular culture, our obsession turned to what we *weren't* rather than what we wanted to be. Consider the defining music of the era – grunge – and the very specific rejection of the excesses of the '80s music that it embodied. Sure, the young adults who were propelling this movement still consumed more mainstream, accessible, and familiar entertainment, too, but they did it in a more "meta" way, to use the vernacular of the time. They watched the fluffy soap opera *Beverly Hills, 90210*, but they watched it so that they could talk about it and mock it afterward, not because they were deeply, empathetically absorbed in the characters and narrative. As surely as flannel had replaced Spandex, willing suspension of disbelief had given way to ironic detachment. The '90s gave us *Titanic* and *The Lion King*, yes, but they also gave us *Pulp Fiction* and *Trainspotting* and, for the cool kids who set the pop culture agenda, there was more social currency in the latter than the former, by far.

Up the street at your friendly neighbourhood ad agency, they viewed this unexpected transformation with mixed feelings. On the one hand, it meant that there was suddenly too much risk in selling brands in the context of lifestyle and aspiration, and nothing obvious to replace that tactic. This was scary to Madison Avenue, because that had always been their best trick. Now, the whole idea of aspiration seemed old-fashioned – abhorrent, even – and it looked as if people were actually working at avoiding being pigeonholed into any handy lifestyle stereotype. The once vast tribal herds of consumers that roamed the earth had disintegrated into hundreds of millions of random individuals who seemed to be trying very hard not to belong. The time-tested strategy of selling to us by showing us a more perfect version of ourselves was suddenly worse than useless. It was dangerous.

On the other hand, though, a lot of creative types in the advertising business saw this as a chance to break out. The very same black-clad young aesthetes who were producing ads were also among the most enthusiastic consumers of alternative culture. (I was pretty sure for a while there in the late '90s that our local barber was giving group discounts to ad agency crea-tive people for the *Trainspotting* haircut and dye job.) This post-modern sensibility was very close to home for them – close enough that they could convince themselves that they, in all their double tall latte–swilling glory, were just like consumers. Finally, they could cast aside the shackles of old-school ad thinking and give the people what they surely wanted: ads that were as cool and funny and ironic and mocking as everything else people were watching, listening to, and talking about. If vain persua-sion could no longer weasel a brand into our hearts, they hoped maybe pop culture awesomeness could.

Either way you chose to look at it, the social transforma-tion of the '90s made life more complicated for brands. The advertising business had to radically improve its cultural surveil-lance apparatus, and to focus it more on what we were doing than on what we desired. They knew that we might never again buy into the lovely but synthetic sentiment of advertising as it had been and would insist instead on some version of rock-solid reality. Even if it was cynical, and even if it wasn't pretty. Meanwhile, the consumers whose approval marketers most wanted were loathe to be caught buying into marketing of any kind. Even the cool, funny, ironic, and mocking kind. We became a moving target, and the game became fast-paced and ever-changing. Cyberpunk author and media theorist Douglas Rushkoff wrote extensively on this change as it was unfolding. Talking in this case about marketing to young people, he said: "Once a teen has been identified as part of the 'target market,' he knows he's done for. The object of the game is to confound the marketers, and keep one's own, authentic culture from show-ing up at the shopping mall as a prepackaged corporate product."

That's what changed. We weren't judging brands on the basis of their quality or value any more, or even at all. We weren't just choosing whether or not to buy, or whether or not to wear a badge of some corporation's making. We weren't even choosing brands in order to buy into an aspirational fantasy, ours or anybody else's. We consumers were now judging brands at least partly on the basis of their social meaning in the here and now. Brands suddenly found themselves very badly wanting our approval almost independently of the products they were selling. It was as if they wanted to be like us, more than for us to be like them. Some brands took it further, actually trying to *be* cool, that most elusive of all cultural prizes. (The results tended to be mixed and ephemeral: Nike, for example, often succeeded, using Beatles music and stars like Michael Jordan; Pepsi often did not, using a little too much neon and stars like MC Hammer.) The more elusive and difficult it became to impress the cool kids, the harder brands tried to suck up to us. After all, this was still marketing. There was still stuff to be sold. And after all, as Rushkoff put it, "A person who is striving not to strive is striving nonetheless." For brands, striving is where the money is.

For consumers, the effect of all this was innocuous enough. Pleasant, even. Ads got more entertaining and less bombastic. It gave us another reason to watch the Super Bowl. We enjoyed the constant supply of amusing memes to share at the office ("Whassuuuup!!!"). We laughed, so the ad biz thought it was on to something and kept it up. But, for the corporate marketing machine, this fundamentally – and unintentionally – altered the process of branding. For one thing, there had been casualties in the quest for coolness. Several iconic brands – Levi's and McDonald's and American Express and Reebok – ended the '90s with much less street cred than they'd had when the decade began. Where once marketers invented brands in the sanctity of their Madison Avenue towers and then tried them out in the marketplace, many now found that they had to go to the marketplace first or risk irrelevance. Market research became more about trying to understand people and less about testing things on them. In the ad agency world, this need created a whole new job. *My* old job, as a matter of fact: the strategic planner, a person whose primary responsibility was to stalk consumers in search of some kind of common psychological ground on which a brand could hope to gain their approval. A few even coined the title "cool hunter" for themselves, so desperately did brands want to stay in this cultural game over which they had lost control. Advertising had always been, and largely still was, the tip of the spear for brands, but the focus of its work had changed from creation to surveillance.

When the smoke cleared, we consumers found ourselves in a radically different role in our relationship with brands. Before the '90s, the marketplace had been like a classroom. The marketer taught, his brand was the lesson, and the students were expected to sit quietly, take notes, and leave the room knowing something they didn't know before. They could choose to act on what they'd learned or not, but that was kind of it. After the '90s, though, the marketplace became more like a theatre. The marketer stood on stage, his brand was the main attraction, and the people watching were an audience upon whose reaction – both during and after the performance – the future of his business depended. Brands needed our approval. Desperately. We had stopped being mere targets and had become an auditorium full of skeptics sitting back, arms crossed, chanting, "Here we are, now. Entertain us."

That's how advertising's *coup de grâce* was delivered – by consumers. Half a century after *The Hidden Persuaders*, the tables had really, finally turned. We had become critically influential in the process of branding, because brand marketers, deprived of the power to set the cultural agenda, were increasingly taking their cues from us.

The only problem was, we didn't realize they were paying any attention.

————

Here's the best thing that ever happened to me in a focus group.

For those fortunate souls unfamiliar with the term "focus group," here's a primer: A market research company, acting on behalf of a marketer, telephones random but similar consumers until they have assembled eight or ten people willing to spend two hours in a room together talking about whatever that marketer is hoping to say or sell. These people show up at a research company facility at the appointed hour, are fed sandwiches, cookies, and coffee or soft drinks, and participate in a discussion led by a professional moderator whose job it is to get them to speak frankly. They do so for a prescribed period of time and then, if they behave, they are given envelopes of cash as they leave at the end of the evening. Meanwhile, their discussion is observed by marketing professionals seated in an adjacent room, watching the proceedings through a one-way glass and hoping for some kind of eureka moment that will reveal just what the hell it is consumers are thinking. The people having the discussion, absurdly, know that they're being observed, though not necessarily by whom. There, surrounded by total strangers, buzzing from caffeine and sugar, and being watched by faceless entities like a suspect on *Cold Case*, each is expected to reveal his or her innermost feelings for the commercial benefit of the company that paid for the sandwiches.

That, more or less, is a focus group.

In the late '90s, my firm was conducting research like this on behalf of some brands in the brewing industry. Their concern was that beer was losing its incumbent coolness among young people, who were more often choosing cocktails and even wine than they were suds (clubbing was replacing keggers for the social college-aged young adult, and I guess nobody had so far invented a crantini hat). Meanwhile, the now aging demographic who had made beer the giant industry it is were also either abandoning it or drinking it in less copious quantities because it made them feel bloaty. These two shifts in drinking habits together spelled a drop in sales volume that was scaring the whole brewing industry. Our goal was to try to figure out whether there was some other place in people's lives that beer could fit and some other social currency we could give it, in the hope of getting more people to keep and consume beer in their homes the way they seemed to be doing with wine.

This particular focus group was composed entirely of men who seemed to be outgrowing beer and were therefore an urgent target for our attention. As I sat dutifully observing their interaction from the other side of the glass, the men munched on cookies and sipped coffee and held forth on the fine art of matching beverages to foods, the role beer plays in a life well lived, and the underappreciated magic of a well-toasted hop. About an hour into the discussion, the door of the observation room where I was sitting opened, and a smartly dressed woman strode in and took the seat beside me. Arms crossed, she peered intently at the group just as I was doing. She seemed so

43

confident in her right to be there that I just assumed she was from the research company, or maybe someone from the client's organization whom I'd not yet met. That is, until she flung her chair backwards on its wheels, threw her arms in the air, and said, a little too loudly, "He's lying! He's a big, fat lying sack of *crap*!"

You don't hear that a lot in focus groups, on either side of the glass. Not out loud, anyway.

After a couple of people from the research facility escorted the woman out of the room, I learned that she was, in fact, the wife of one of the participants in the focus group. It wasn't clear whether she was drunk when she arrived or had gone to a nearby pub to tip a few during the focus group, but she had wandered in from the waiting room where her husband had left her while he earned them $75 by helping to guide the strategy of Canada's multibillion dollar brewing industry. The worst part is, I think she might have been right. I think her drunken outburst might have had more truth in it than anything being said by eight posturing men who didn't know each other but wanted to make a good impression.

The crucial point is that corporations today are by nature much more often reactive than they are proactive when it comes to marketing. They rarely have very much imagination or any incentive to acquire it. For most companies, most of the time, what drives their behaviour is the collection of signals they receive about what works and what does not. These signals are key to an ongoing pursuit of efficiency, not creativity. They take guesswork out of the marketing process, and they reduce risk, something corporations hate. They're listening in order to avoid mistakes, to minimize wasted effort and maximize the return on marketing dollars. One of the ways companies pick up these signals is by doing "qualitative" research like this. And if I could afford to pay everybody in the world $75 to not participate in this kind of research ever again, I would.

Believe it or not, you don't want to live in a world where brand marketers act according to what you tell them in face-to-face market research. When marketers use statistically valid surveys, that's fair game, because there is some science to those and the sheer number of people being polled generally washes out distracting subjectivity. They're like political polls. When marketers monitor our actual behaviour as shoppers by measuring sales, that's fair game, too, because that information is honest and commercially useful in terms of building good businesses. As we plunk our money down, we are telling the absolute truth, and we actually want to be heard. But when we're asked to talk in abstract terms about the brands in our lives in front of a bunch of strangers and pseudo-scientists, the risk that we'll tell some dangerous lies is too great.

It's not that we're liars by nature, mind you. However, two very powerful forces are at work in a focus group setting that conspire to make us less than truthful:

The first is the simple fact that we're in a group when we're being asked to make these intimate confessions. We tend to avoid talking about certain subjects in group settings, especially if that group is composed of people we don't know. Religion, politics, sex, money, personal hygiene, that sort of thing. Put us in a group and raise one of those topics, and nine times out of ten we'll keep our cards pretty close to our vests (the tenth time, we'll fight like weasels, get mean and personal, and go home angry and hurt, which makes for entertaining – but unproductive – focus groups). Some people feel the same way about many of the things they buy. They won't be forthright about why they chose a particular brand of toothpaste, because they don't want to argue about their choice with strangers who chose differently. They also don't want, in the process, to look vain, lazy, or gullible. Place eight or ten people like that in a room, and what you'll end up with is consensus on the inarguable facts and little else. What makes that dangerous? Well, from the other side of the one-way glass, a group like that makes a marketer think that people aren't that engaged in his brand, or in the idea of brands at all. At best, he might think the only way to win market share is by making his product cheaper. When that happens, big marketers win and get bigger, since they have the scale to cut costs, while small ones bleed to death because of shrinking profit margins. The consumer ends up with less choice. At worst, this kind of feedback might tempt the marketer to think about how to cut his product's price by reducing its quality, since we don't seem to care anyway. The fruit of that logic fills the tables at garage sales, and occasionally the front pages of newspapers when a product is recalled for spontaneously catching fire or poisoning kids with lead-infused paint. When an untruthful consumer meets a cynical, opportunistic marketer, the results can be toxic.

The second force at work here is that we're being asked to *speculate* about our own behaviour as consumers. If some guy with hipster glasses and a goatee asks me how I plan to buy my next vacuum cleaner, and seven strangers turn and look at me to hear my answer, I am not going to say, "I'll pick the coolest looking one, check to see if the brand name is famous or not, wait until it's on sale, and bam! Buy it." Even though, for me, this would be true. No, I'm going to lie. I'm going to tell him that I plan to do lots of research and homework, comparison shop carefully, visit on-line vacuum cleaner forums and consult

my neighbours, weigh the information carefully against my specific needs, and choose my machine accordingly. It's simply not
reasonable to ask me to be honest and accurate in predicting
my own behaviour (I also swore I would lose ten pounds this
year) even in private, never mind in front of my new focus group
buddies. My answer is going to be clouded by good intentions,
a desire to please, the need to win the respect of the other sand-
wich-eaters, and my own ego.

How dangerous could this be? Back on the other side of
that one-way glass, the marketer listening to my answer is con-
cluding that what it takes to sell his product is information. It
has to be great on paper, he will decide, that's all that matters.
At best, that leads to uniformly dull, competent products but,
again, no real choice; at worst, this false objectivity leads to
manipulative rhetoric and even product compromises that make
a brand look good on paper but aren't really in our best interest. Think mutual fund annual returns, or automobile horsepower, for example, two product categories where awful
products can generate impressive advertising claims.

Much as this might seem like a simple indictment of focus
groups, I think the implications of bad signals are much broader
and more fundamental. The surveillance apparatus of marketers
includes some tools that are fraught with peril for us all, because
they discourage us from telling the truth, even to ourselves.
Asking the wrong questions and getting less than the truth in
response makes good companies do stupid things, and bad companies do evil ones. For consumers, that means two things: First,
we can't let the only signals corporations get from us be through
channels they control. We can't answer only the questions they
ask and otherwise remain petulantly silent. We have to engage.
We have to make sure that we're sending signals on our own

agenda, in our own channels, so that their data is mostly composed of what is spontaneous, personal, and true. (In the final chapters, I'll talk more about how we can do that.)

Second, we've got to try to be more honest with ourselves about what we want and the choices we make. Even the most vile, cynical, and manipulative corporation still wants satisfied, or at least tolerant, customers. They need them to survive. But they will never care more than we do. They won't give us more than we ask for. They won't say anything we don't accept. They will use their brands to make us look and feel the way we say we want to look and feel. Like some jerk in a bar trying to attract the amorous attention of a stranger, they'll cast morality aside in favour of whatever seems to get us smiling, talking, and laughing. And that has a way of setting the tone for the whole relationship.

For crying out loud, let's not lead them on.

———

If German marketing has one defining characteristic, it's the arrogance of its brands. Its most famous marketers are much more likely to tell us what we want rather than to ask, and this is often, perversely, the source of their appeal. Yet, in the spring of 2009, when BMW rolled out the second generation of its Z4 roadster, it revealed to the world a car that was less, not more, daringly styled than its predecessor. A car that was, by comparison to its radical and controversial namesake, conventionally pretty. Although technologically advanced from the car BMW first introduced in 2002 to replace the quirky Z3, from a design point of view the updated Z4 was a giant, deliberate step backwards.

You would think that if any car company had the ability to be a tastemaker, it would be BMW. Its sporty sedans had been design benchmarks for the biggest car companies in the world since at least the 1980s. Their brand had swaggered its way to yuppie stardom in that decade, taking its place as an icon of aspiration alongside Rolex watches and American Express Gold Cards. Unlike the brash arrogance of brands like Porsche or Mercedes-Benz, though, BMW had managed to avoid at least some of the negative social meaning that goes with luxury brands while being universally recognizable as a status symbol. All the while, they managed both to keep growing (they are today more than ten times the size of, say, Porsche, thanks partly to a broader product offering) and to be profitable (their profit margins on each unit sold have consistently been among the highest in the industry for many years). BMW somehow pulled off the neat marketing trick of being both prestigious and attainable, and that's given them a lot of influence in the car world. So who better to lead us into the future of car design? Who better to tell us what coolness on four wheels is going to look like next year, or five years down the road?

That's the way BMW saw it, too, when they made American-born Chris Bangle their Chief of Design back in 1992. With the car business's long product cycles, it would take some time before Bangle's vision would truly be expressed in the BMW product line. But Bangle had a vision, all right, and he had his Board's full support to, as one Board member would later put it, "map out a clear and aesthetic route [for BMW] into the future." Although not the first total redesign to happen under his leadership, the Z4 was probably the purest declaration of where Bangle thought that future lay. And the BMW faithful hated it.

To many eyes, the Z4 was uglier than the box it came in. Another automotive designer said it appeared to have been "designed with a machete." It was wrapped in strange, dissonant creases, oddly proportioned with a ludicrously long hood and a stumpy trunk, and festooned with self-consciously modern details. The Z4 seemed to be flipping the bird at the very idiom of a roadster, and certainly at the people who loved the car it was replacing. Attending a launch party for the Z4, I was struck by the way it seemed to sit there silently mocking anybody who didn't get it. People stared at the car in a mild state of shock and muttered to each other the way people must have done on first seeing Warhol's soup cans.

And so began a war. In Munich, one car after another was redesigned with at least some of the design themes declared by the Z4. Meanwhile, on Internet forums, Bangle's name became a pejorative verb (as in, "the new 5-series has been thoroughly Bangled"), and terms like Bangle Butt were coined to describe recurring design features in his work. Patient and defiant, the powers that be at BMW continued to try to evolve past what they considered the company's stodgy design tradition, Teutonically certain they would change our tastes. And increasingly sarcastic and cranky, BMW enthusiasts pronounced the demise of a great brand, pouting that if BMW was going to design its cars to appeal to the masses, they might as well head to the nearest Lexus dealer for their next ride.

In the end, despite the fact that its market share had grown, BMW blinked. When the hot-selling but controversial 7-series came due for mid-cycle freshening, Bangle's trademark rear end was minimized. When the popular 3-series was redesigned, the edgy creases disappeared, and the new car looked like a sleek, purified version of the *pre*-Bangle model. Eventually, in February

2009, Chris Bangle left BMW and the car business in search of new design frontiers. And in May, the new Z4 went on sale, complete with luscious curves and a return to more traditional BMW roadster proportions. There were no *mea culpas*, but it seems reasonable to speculate that the company knew it couldn't risk alienating the enthusiasts of their brand for much longer. A product doesn't have prestige just because its maker says so; it has it because *we* say so. In the case of BMW, that status is conferred by car nuts. Those people sent a very clear, strong signal to the company that their products had to look like BMWs to keep that status, no matter what the unwashed masses might think.

Even Germans couldn't argue with that.

We like to think that corporations will do whatever they can get away with. In some ways, I guess it's true. Profit will always be the difference between what a product costs to make and what we think it's worth, so every marketer has an abiding interest in what we'll tolerate. But what really drives most corporate behaviour is not discovering the limits of our tolerance, it's discovering what works: what gets them what they want. Like every successfully evolved beast in creation, they will observe what works and do more of it, and they will observe what does not work and do less of it. BMW wants two things: it wants to sell ever more cars, and it wants to preserve its prestige so that we'll pay more for them. With their bold design experiments, they accomplished only one of those objectives. The one you might think matters the most. And yet, despite selling lots of cars, despite the enormous development and tooling costs of creating a new one, despite the tremendous amount of corporate ego invested in these products and the very high visibility of them, and despite the stupendous investment of marketing know-how and dollars, consumers were apparently able to change BMW's agenda anyway. By making sure that what they were doing didn't work.

Stories like this one, or like the much more famous failed 1985 launch of New Coke, are more complex than a simple matter of people not buying a product they don't like. We consumers have the power to grant or withhold the choice not only to buy a product, but also to approve of its brand, to give it social meaning, and to endorse and promote it to our peers. The same surveillance apparatus that stalks us for opportunities to sell picks up even more loudly any hint that we're not feeling the love any more. And the fewer functional differences there are between one brand and another – say, between a 3-series BMW and a Toyota Camry, not to put too fine a point on this – the more carefully those signals are monitored. The absence of differences between brands doesn't make fools of consumers; it makes us infinitely more powerful. Because, without them, that marketer's brand is all they've got. It keeps them needing us just a little more than we need them.

Heady stuff.

Still, before we start limbering up our typing fingers and firing off vitriolic on-line diatribes against our cellphone carriers, we can't let ourselves forget how keenly accomplished these corporate beasts are at qualifying our signals. They know which ones matter and which ones do not, which ones might cost them money and which ones are merely a little short-lived embarrassment. The rhetoric of the faithful was effective in the BMW case, but that doesn't mean that rhetoric alone always does the job. If it's not attached to leverage, if it can't hit them where it hurts, the corporate beast will simply be deaf to it. The beast, you see, is not the malevolent, omnipotent mastermind we sometimes fear it is. For consumers, at least, it's actually something much more primitive and predictable.

———

In 2003, riding a fashionable wave of anti-marketing activism, a documentary film appeared on the festival circuit, entitled *The Corporation*. It was critically acclaimed and became a darling of the no-logoists because of its clever central thesis: Corporations, it argued, are psychopaths. If a typical corporate enterprise were a person, its behaviour would be considered criminally dangerous by society's standards. The profit-driven corporation, it smugly asserted, is a perfect analog for a clinically diagnosed psychopath.

True? Well, sort of. The corporation is not a psychopath, or at least no more so than a cow, a dog, or an ocelot is. What ocelots and psychopaths and corporations all have in common is singularity of purpose: they selfishly act on natural urges to survive and prosper at all costs. Beyond this, though, the comparison doesn't hold much water. Pyschopaths are popularly characterized as bad guys, and in clinical terms, they are partly defined by their inability to learn from past mistakes. Neither is generally true of corporations. All corporations want to do is make money, because that's all their numerous stakeholders – labour, management, and investors – can agree on. That, by default, is their purpose. No corporation I've ever worked with explicitly includes a commitment to evil in its mission statement; there wouldn't be any money in it (even biker gangs depend ultimately on satisfied customers to sustain themselves). And corporations are, in their way, generally good at learning from their pasts, as long as the lessons have to do with profit. They remember what worked. Yes, they can be blind to the consequences of what they do to survive – also true of cows, dogs, and ocelots – and they don't always adapt to their environments fast enough. But this doesn't make them evil. It just makes them beasts. To a consumer, a corporation is better and more productively thought of as a giant, dull-witted organism, selfishly and narrowly preoccupied with its ecological destiny. A corporation is not Hannibal Lecter. It is a cow.

This notion obviously tends to invite argument. What I've noticed, though, is that the arguments don't cite corporations as entities, but rather individuals within them, and most especially their leaders. Fair enough. But just as there are evil corporate executives, so are there evil plumbers, clerics, piano teachers, baristas, and, I'm pretty sure, the dry cleaner who shrinks my shirt collars. The fact of evil practitioners does not impugn the legitimacy of an occupation. If an evil executive lands a job in a corporation, it's because the corporation narrowly saw the potential for profit in hiring that executive. That's *all* it saw, because it is a big, dumb animal. I'd submit that Warren Buffett could wear a tutu to the office and spend his days picking the wings off flies, and the shareholders of Berkshire Hathaway would look right past it as long as he was getting results. Because results are all that that organism and the system that sustains it understand. Berkshire Hathaway, too, is a cow.

The truth of this came home for me while working on this very chapter. One morning, I paused for a break from the keyboard and took a long walk, eventually finding myself in a busy Starbucks at the corner of Allen and Delancey in Manhattan's Lower East Side. The area is a historic hotbed of New York cultural and political radicalism, but you'd never know it from inside this Starbucks. Not even from the handful of sullenly vague archival photos on the wall, all of which put together might equal in size just one of the faux-retro European tourism posters promoting dark roasted coffee. You'd never know that in 2005, citizens of this storied and feisty pocket of New York City were up in arms about the "sinister" coffee brand bullying its way into the neighbourhood. "The fourth horseman of the Apocalypse," grumped one blogger, "is riding into the Lower East Side." The rhetoric was about as heated as these things get, and the incursion was held up by some of the freedom fighters as evidence that "New York City [was] slowly being turned into a shopping mall." Starbucks went ahead and built the store here anyway. Why? Because they're evil? Bent on prostituting urban café culture or destroying the authenticity of a piece of cultural history? I doubt it. I think Starbucks probably just knew that there were a lot of people on the Lower East Side who would buy their coffee. To them, the rest was just noise.

The corporate beast doesn't go looking for resistance, believe me. The corporation is a cow, and it's a very pragmatic cow. It will dedicate its energy to whatever works and assiduously avoid wasting it on anything that doesn't. So, if we want to make a difference, we can never forget what "works" means to a cow. The distinction between signal and noise in the branded marketing game is leverage. Leverage means money to spend, or it means the power to influence the commercial value of a corporation's brand. In more ways than just the obvious one, you get what you pay for in this world. More loudly than all the bloggers on the Internet, your money is always talking. As long as someone is paying, those cows will keep producing.

And as we'll see in the next chapter, that leverage begins long before we even think about heading to the mall.

CHAPTER THREE

"LADIES AND GENTLEMEN, THE BEATLES!"

Think of Bob Garfield as the Al Gore of brands.

If you don't know who Bob Garfield is, that just means you don't work in advertising. Garfield is a columnist for *Advertising Age*, the industry's quasi-biblical trade paper. Until 2010, his usual stock-in-trade was the reviewing of advertising campaigns, about which he wrote acerbically and sometimes with biting – and usually justified – sarcasm. He is a guy who seems to think that branded marketing matters, but that it's often practised by people who aren't very bright. In April of 2005, though, Garfield paused to change the subject. He wrote a piece for *Ad Age* called "The Chaos Scenario: A Look at the Marketing Industry's Coming Disaster." This new theme dominated his writing from that day to this, becoming the topic of a similarly titled book in 2009. The essence of his thesis: branded marketing is going to be royally screwed by rapid and massive changes in the media universe, enough so that its very survival is debatable. Three television networks, a few radio stations, and a newspaper or two for each community have been replaced by a blizzard of media content carried by numerous technologies. Taken together, the matrix of stuff to watch, read, and listen to, and the growing variety of devices to do it with, produces so many options that I'm actually stumped for a metaphor. E-mail me if you have any ideas.

This, of course, is hardly news. We're all well aware of media's increasing ubiquity – we're soaking in it, as that old Palmolive dishwashing detergent commercial put it – and one might even imagine that it's been a boon to advertisers. So how could it actually threaten the future of branded marketing? Inside the ad world, the debate centres around two big and very fashionable themes. One is the creative challenge of getting our attention amid this cacophonous din. The other is the impact of social media, such as Facebook and Twitter, and the new opportunity, expectation, and duty that they present to marketers to listen to consumers, rather than just to talk at us. All well and good. Yes, brands have to try harder to be noticed, and yes, brands have to listen to consumers now. Yet the true nature of the threat isn't the change in the relationship between brands and consumers in the media, it's the fact that the relationship is becoming very uneconomical. The problem boils down to simple arithmetic: with a hundred times as many ways to interact with media, but not a hundred times as many people interacting with each one, individual audiences are smaller. A lot smaller.

Here's why that matters.

If we lived a life in which we only bought what we needed, and we always knew what that was, this would all be moot. Brands would be many fewer and not very meaningful. Advertising would not exist. Commerce would be more about making and distributing products, and much less about selling them. But we don't live that life and, in fact, we take some nationalistic pride in our economy being driven by demand and choice rather than by production management. Most of us want more than we absolutely need and, harnessed properly, that collective desire can be and sometimes has been a powerful force for innovation and economic development. It's on that truth that the marketing world is premised and sustains itself, for better and for worse. Charles Kettering, an inventor and head of research for General Motors from 1920 to 1947, once put it this way: "The key to economic prosperity is the organized creation of dissatisfaction." Chillingly cynical but essentially true. Before you object too strongly, bear in mind that you owe Mr. Kettering the electric starter and the air conditioner in your car. The line between needing and wanting, as ever, is a movable and subjective thing.

For most of modern history, the key to the organized creation of dissatisfaction has been mass media, and the king of them all was television. Marketers have used TV to advertise to us directly and to familiarize us with their brands, while the people who create the entertainment content we watch have compulsively and relentlessly presented stories about people who are better looking and more interesting than us, and have more money and better stuff. In the age of mass media, that had two massive benefits for the branded marketing process. One was that it was easy to create consensus about what aspiration looked like. If fifteen million people were watching *L.A. Law* every week, it was quick, easy work to get America nodding that Bäumler suits were pretty nice. The second was that it turned selling into a numbers game. If millions of people saw an ad, the marketer only needed to convert a small percentage of them in order to sell a lot of suits. Like the Grand Banks cod or the plains buffalo of yore, there were so many targets that any brand with enough money to play the game would be hard pressed to go home hungry. To understand the sheer scale of bombardment that was possible only a few decades ago, consider this: By the time Ed Sullivan introduced North America to the Beatles in 1964, his show had for years regularly attracted half of all the television viewers in the land. *Half!* His wasn't the only show at the time that could do it, either. Corporations had the whip hand because they controlled the content and the channels of distribution, which were both conveniently scarce. Even better for them, that scarcity made television, by definition, a communal experience for us.

In that environment, the enormous cost of producing a prime-time soap opera made sense. An eight- or nine-figure advertising budget made sense. The hundreds of thousands of dollars it cost to make a television commercial made sense. The six-figure salary of a copywriter or the five-figure day rate of a commercial director made sense, or at least was too minor to notice compared to the millions of dollars flying around, or the millions of people watching those sitcoms and ads together. But change that environment, and suddenly the rest of it doesn't make any sense at all. And change it did. By the end of the '70s, the top-rated programs on television drew audiences half the size of Ed's. By the end of the '90s, less than half that again. Cable, then home video, and finally other screens altogether, fragmented audiences and made marketing much harder work. Today, a high-profile show like *Mad Men* qualifies as a pop culture sensation with a mere two million or so viewers, if you count repeats. As Joni Mitchell put it, "You don't know what you've got 'til it's gone." Today, now that marketers can't take big audiences for granted, there is nothing they lust for more.

More than any other single force acting on branded marketing, I think this disintegration of audiences was responsible for initiating the power shift from marketer to consumer. It happened so slowly that we didn't even notice it: Broadcast television was joined by cable; then by a lot more cable; then, time-shifting devices like those VCRs with the flashing 12:00; then, home video; then, the Internet in all its YouTube glory; and on and on. As each successive technology added more choices, those choices became more narrow and specific in their appeal (the idea of a television network dedicated entirely to, say, the biographies of famous dead people would have seemed like an absurd waste of precious bandwidth in Ed's time). The shift happened over four decades, so on any given Sunday night for any given generation, the choices in front of us just seemed normal. Choice didn't land on us like an anvil. It washed over us slowly, inexorably.

For a long time, branded marketers didn't pay much attention to the change, either, and when they did I'm sure they wanted to keep it quiet. After all, when there was very little choice in media, and when those media were consumed passively and were under the control of the corporations who funded them, marketers could treat us as one giant, homogenous herd of potential customers whose lives would all be equally improved by this drain cleaner or that tiger in our tank. Whereas today, with almost infinite choice in media, we're substantially in charge of what we see, hear, and read, and of when we do so. We have control. Individually. There's a reason why one of the first things to happen in a political *coup d'état* is the forcible seizure of media outlets. A junta not only wants to limit freedom of speech, it also wants to limit the freedom of choice. To remain in control, the junta needs everybody in the same place at the same time, watching and hearing the same thing.

That's why Garfield's *Chaos Scenario* matters. All this fragmentation that's scaring the pants off marketers and undermining the economics of the media industry is also creating a bedrock foundation for the consumer republic, because it means that branded marketing can't take its customers for granted any more. We live in an era when the idea of having to be home at 8:00 p.m. on Sunday night to watch your favourite show seems as quaint as starting your car with a hand crank. An era when a grainy home video of a cat playing the piano can outperform the viewer numbers for a mid-season episode of *CSI Miami*. An era when brands are paying more than six times – *in inflation-adjusted dollars* – what they did forty years ago for each Super Bowl viewer. To marketers, the consumer has suddenly become a valuable and slightly frightening creature indeed. Viewers, readers, and listeners have become as scarce as albino gorillas.

Big, scary albino gorillas with credit cards and remote controls.

Which reminds me of a story.

In 1995, the World Wide Web was little more than a curiosity to the few people who'd paid any attention to its arrival, and that certainly included those of us who worked in advertising. The web was barely two years old, and it consisted mainly of text, hyperlinks, and the occasional tiny pixelated image that took minutes to load. There wasn't much to be seen out there – the number of web pages worldwide was said to be in the tens of thousands at the most – and what there was to see was so agonizingly slow to access that I'm sure it was only the need to justify those multi-thousand-dollar personal computers that kept people trying at all.

Against that primitive backdrop, imagine this. An engineering student had assembled an electric model train set at a university somewhere in Germany – Bremen, as I recall (there's no trace of the story left on the Web). The train set could not only be viewed on the Web from anywhere in the world in real time (or as real as it gets at 14.4 kbps), but it could also be *operated* via the web. You could go to the little train's web page, click your mouse on buttons that made the train go, stop, and reverse, and then watch it happen all the way across the Atlantic Ocean at any time of the day or night. Admittedly a breathless early adopter of the web in all its glacial splendour, I sought meaning in every absurd experiment that I stumbled on, and this one was no different. There was, I was certain, Something Happening Here. Or, to be more precise, I guess, in Bremen. In any case, history in the making is meant to be shared. I flagged down a passing colleague to thrill him with this glimpse of the future.

"Dude, you have to check this out."

He sauntered over to my desk (ad agency creative types only saunter, ever) and peered into the computer monitor with that expression you sometimes see on dogs watching TV. With a flourish, I clicked "Go." A minute passed. I refreshed the page. And again. And again. Until finally, on the fourth try, the grainy little picture of the train had become a blur. It was moving. Or probably, anyway. I looked at him triumphantly, expecting to see his eyes widen in amazement and my own credentials as a seer enshrined once and for all. In this, I was disappointed. He expressed some doubt that there would ever be much of a market for remotely controlling other people's model trains from thousands of miles away. But I was stoked. Yes, okay, a little bit because you could control other people's model trains from thousands of miles away, but also because, once again, humanity had asserted its relentless demand for autonomy. The paint was hardly dry on the shiny new World Wide Web, and somebody out there was already using it to make stuff happen not for the purpose of meeting some kind of functional need but for the sheer joy of it.

When people write about media in the twentieth century, the story always seems to revolve around technology. The generally accepted version of events is that technological innovation presented us with choices we had never had before, and we adapted ourselves to that climate of choice by becoming choosy. The more options and conveniences laid out before us on the buffet of modernism, the more voracious and varied our consumption became. Certainly, from a corporate point of view, that's how it must have seemed. There wasn't much doubt in Hollywood or Silicon Valley which was the chicken and which was the egg. But the truth, I think, is quite different. The truth is that, probably since the dawn of history, we've all been tapping our feet impatiently waiting for the future to happen. I think the corporate/scientific/industrial complex has been scrambling to catch up with our collective vision, which has almost unfailingly been more vivid and daring than theirs.

Over and over again, as an agent of branded marketing, I've seen it with my own eyes. For example, the cable company I worked with in the late '90s spent a handsome sum on research to figure out how to package cable channels so that government regulations would be met, the cable company would make money, and the consumer would be happy, or at least tolerant. And what did those consumers want? They wanted to know where the heck video-on-demand was. A technology that was still years in the future; an urge that would create businesses from YouTube to TiVo. Before that, I advised a cellular phone company. Again, vast tracts of market research were prepared, this time in an effort to figure out how to make pagers appealing to young people. And what did those young people demand? It's fine to get text messages on this thing, they said, but what's the point if you can't reply? Years later, when the first BlackBerry was introduced, not many marketers saw the potential of the product for anyone beyond real estate agents and stockbrokers, unless they'd been listening to those consumers for whom the idea of answering a text-based message was as obvious and natural as breathing. Before that, back at Panasonic, I was there when the first CD players were presented to consumers in focus groups. We thought we were replacing the vinyl record and the turntable and that we'd get around to replacing the cassette tape next. Yet, on being exposed to this new marvel, what did consumers want? They wanted to know why you couldn't record on these shiny discs, too.

Our impatience with the future predates the digital age by a long shot, in fact, and our media consumption has always been a target for it. As evidence, I'm fond of citing the story of the invention of the first wireless remote control – the Zenith Space Command – the handiwork of Robert Adler, an engineer at Zenith Radio Corporation. Why? Because Adler managed this feat in 1956, when most Americans were lucky to have three television stations from which to choose. It's hard to imagine that a remote control – a *wireless* remote control at that – would be the answer to any sort of pressing consumer problem when there were only two other choices besides the one you were watching, and the opportunity to choose only occurred every thirty or sixty minutes. But it turns out that, although the Space Command was the first wireless remote for a television set, even it wasn't our first attempt to control a media experience without getting out of our chairs. That honour goes to the hilariously named Philco Mystery Control, born in 1939, as a device to control your family *radio*.

Consider what seems to have been the inevitability of that trivial piece of technology, and it won't surprise you to learn that the "clicker" became a symbol of the greatest danger the branding world would ever and always face: the autonomous urges of the media consumer. When remote controls became common, ad agency types used them as threats to make clients agree to buy more entertaining and elaborate advertising ideas. "You don't want to get zapped," creative types would solemnly intone, while sliding military procurement-sized production estimates across the table. When VCRs became common, it was the fast-forward button that embodied this terrible fear. When personal video recorders like TiVo became common, the ease with which we consumers could avoid branded communication was the stuff of nightmares (and with good reason, since various industry sources now put the percentage of commercials "zapped" by TiVo and other PVR users at anywhere from 75 to 90 per cent). Just as surely as kids everywhere set their new toys aside and play instead with the boxes they came in, we are by our very nature driven to be in control of our experience.

What splintered mass media into a million fragments, in the process making audiences so valuable to marketers, was the determined autonomy of those audiences and the competition among marketers to satisfy them. It wasn't luck, it was rarely manipulative genius, and it was only incidentally a gift of technology. What made it happen was our own determination to get what we want. To play with the box. We weren't handcuffed to our La-Z-Boys while corporate-produced culture was rammed down our throats, or not for long, anyway. We chose what we watched and listened to and read and, in doing that, we moved their money around. What makes that so basic to the idea of a consumer republic is that the more we assert our autonomy, the more choices we get. And the more choices we have, the more effect our autonomy has the next time we assert it. And so on, until finally, one day, marketing might ultimately cease to be a process of corporations shouting at millions in the hope of converting a few, and become one of corporations trying to win the trust of a few so that they, in turn, can influence those millions.

Imagine what that would do to a corporation's marketing motivation. Imagine how it would motivate a corporation to not only take our money but leave us feeling good about the transaction.

It's not always easy to understand the present while it's happening. But if we look at branded marketing over the history of mass media, it's hard not to conclude that it is in the final stages of becoming a truly negotiated process. When Ed Sullivan first lit up North American television screens, our only chance to vote on brands was at the cash register. Now, we have some influence over the entire game, almost from the first move. Our natural urge to be autonomous has left brand marketers chasing us all over the media universe, waving new things to watch, read, and listen to in the hope that we'll pause long enough to watch, read, and listen to their branding messages. In the beginning, this power got us television and radio content for free, and print content for a fraction of what it cost to produce. Now the list of things that that chase has given us is too long and obvious to mention. From TV remote to computer mouse to magical touch screen, whether we intend to or not, we're voting with every click. And with every click, our influence grows.

Which brings me back to the Internet.

It's one thing to let a fox into the hen house; it's quite another to have the fox standing at a podium making an acceptance speech while the hens politely applaud. Yet that's exactly the scene that played out at the 2009 Cannes Lions International Advertising Festival as Steve Ballmer, CEO of Microsoft, accepted the honour of Media Person of the Year. The hens: the glitterati of the advertising world, straining expense accounts to the limit for a few days of self-congratulation on the French Riviera. The fox: Ballmer, speaking for Microsoft, a powerhouse in the new economy that has made it its business to render obsolete exactly the kind of vain silliness the hens are here to celebrate, and to then take their money. These two entities have never been what you'd call natural allies. But 2009 wasn't an ordinary year. With the economy undergoing devastating changes, advertising had taken some mortal blows.

Of course, marketing budgets were cut dramatically, as always happens in a recession. On top of this, though, some very rich brands and product categories very suddenly simply went silent as the business climate threatened their survival. The automobile industry, financial services, and even some retailers were high-profile examples. Ad agencies laid people off in probably unprecedented numbers. The market for media was so bad that television had its worst year ever for advance sales of commercial time, while newspapers and magazines found themselves on a death watch, not just for the duration, but maybe for forever.

So the hens, thinking he might hold the secret to avoiding the deep fryer, asked the Media Person of the Year to give a keynote speech, too, and sat rapt as the Microsoft boss held forth. You can watch the whole thing on YouTube, if you're interested. (You may also enjoy the "Steve Ballmer Going Crazy" video, as have a couple of million people before you, but it will be beside the point and may adversely affect how soberly you consume his Cannes presentation.) To my ears, Ballmer's speech contained essentially two sentences that matter:

Sentence That Matters 1: "All ad possibilities are enabled by worlds of content."

Sentence That Matters 2: "All content will be digital."

What must have made these two sentences so resonant for the hens on that warm June evening on the Riviera was this: Because of all the bad stuff that was happening to the branding business, what money was left for branded marketing was stampeding away from traditional media and heading on-line. Up and down Madison Avenue and around the world, marketers were abandoning traditional mass media and lining up for the chance to spend that money on the Internet. Why? To a marketer, on-line advertising has some attractive qualities in a tough economy. For one thing, the price of admission is much lower. Millions have to be spent before you have any idea if a TV ad campaign has worked, whereas you can get started on-line for next to nothing and know whether you're accomplishing anything in days or even hours. For another, Internet advertising is highly measurable and seems very accountable for itself. No brand manager is going to go to his boss in the middle of an economic meltdown and ask to be allowed to gamble millions on ads in traditional media, not when he can look like a hero by tracking the precise effect of every dollar spent on-line. But what made it most attractive, the thing that made digital converts out of the most dyed-in-the-wool ad guys, was the belief that the Internet was where we had all gone when we stopped watching *Two and a Half Men*. Now as never before, they couldn't live without us, and that meant they had to follow us on-line.

And so they did. By one estimate, $65 billion worth of branding money would make the move to cyberspace in 2009, an amount that nearly equals the total revenue of U.S. television networks and cable companies combined. The general consensus was that this money was never going to go back where it came from. For branded marketing, normal would never be normal again.

Why should you care?

First, the bad news. The Internet is, without a doubt, the most measured media platform that has ever existed. What a website knows about you – where you live, what kind of computer you use, what kind of operating system and browser it has, the IP address of that computer and to whom that address is registered, what site you came from, what you read, how long you spent doing it, and where you went next – would take a lot of people's breath away. Even a modest blogger like myself can access all of this information practically for free. If I were a big corporation, that information would be much more comprehensive. If I were Google, I would have the power to record every site you visited after starting at Google's search page, for the entire duration of your session. This is what Google calls your "clickstream," and it's the key to their ability to rank websites and to make their search results precise, accurate, and relevant. A $65 billion cash injection into that world, enabling more content, more branding, and more of *us*, means that more of our consuming behaviour is going to be subject to surveillance than in Vance Packard's sweatiest nightmare. The web doesn't generally put faces and names to the clickstream, but it knows what we're all doing out there. It knows. Which, though mostly not threatening, is at the very least weird.

But, like everything about the squirmy relationship between brands and consumers, there's a silver lining in that cloud. In fact, it could be the biggest single factor in making the consumer republic a reality. As branded marketing transitions from being an air war to being hand-to-hand combat, the fight has suddenly become a lot fairer, and some significant victory spoils await the consumer.

First, the obsession marketers have with measurement on-line means that our behaviour – what we like, what we do, what we care about – is going to have enormous influence on the way they do business. To a branded marketer, data like this is highly addictive, and in the past it hasn't been very rich or insightful. A marketer made media decisions based on loose correlations between the demographics and the location of a particular audience, and the probability that people matching that description would share certain lifestyle characteristics and preferences. In other words, choosing commercial media properties was a gamble based on probabilities: the probability that someone of your age, sex, income, and address might be watching a certain television show or reading a certain newspaper, and the probability that doing so indicates that you might like, say, golf. Now, on the Internet, that risk is almost gone. There is no ambiguity about what you like. You're telling them with every click, often now in real time. As happy as that might make them, it also produces three pretty great benefits for consumers. First, branded marketers are going to feel more and more compelled to follow and serve our preferences rather than carpet bomb us with ads. The on-line content that attracts their marketing money will be the content we care most about preserving. If it's golf-related content you like, then it's golf-related content you shall have.

Second, our voices are going to be louder than they have ever been. According to the media measurement experts at the

Nielsen Company (the same ones that built their empire counting Ed Sullivan viewers), marketing spending in social media rose 119 per cent in 2009, making it account for about 15 per cent of the money corporations spend to market themselves online. That tells you two things. It tells you that they think it matters to be there, where we're talking to each other. It also tells you that they're listening to what we say, because there's real money at stake. We live in an era in which a single, angry consumer can, with a little luck and determination, David-like, get the undivided attention of a mighty corporation. That wasn't very likely when we had to write letters or call customer service departments. Now, it's inevitable.

Third, the experience we have with brands is going to be observed by lots and lots of people just like us. Here, again, it's the Facebooks and Twitters of the world that are making the biggest difference, something I'll examine more closely in Chapter 9. Today, not only do brand marketers hear us if we love/hate/distrust/are confused by what they sell – or even if all we do is click that little thumbs-down button – but so will other people who share our interests and values. By that very same token, brands are now forced to talk back. In a one-way media universe, brands lectured us about what they had to sell, but they never took questions afterward. That they should be silent when they were not selling was assumed. Now, it's not. Now, we can start the conversation, and brands are going to be judged whether they answer us or not. Discourse between a brand and a single customer is often held in public, like a trial in open court, and the audience observes, learns, takes sides, and acts on how that discourse unfolds. Remember, we don't so much buy products any more as we choose the companies we want to bring them to us. Because it has no secrets, the web can reveal who those companies really are, if we know how to look. Lots of us already do. Many more soon will, at the rate these media are growing audiences.

In the meantime, you can be sure a Red Bull–addled geek is hunched over a laptop at Starbucks right now, somewhere in the world, writing the code that will become the website that will tell us the answer with a click.

Bob Garfield is right. The world *is* in chaos, at least if brands are your business. Nothing is ever going to be the same again, and it's probably not an exaggeration to say that in the coming years branded marketing will be completely reinvented, if it's to survive. Whether marketers like it or not, consumers are going to have a big hand in that reinvention, and that could be the best thing ever to happen to consumerism. Consumers have never had an opportunity before like the one Garfield's chaos scenario has given us. Which is only fitting, since, as any new age philosopher/management guru/inspirational speaker will tell you, "chaos" and "opportunity" go together like love and marriage. In fact, I got fourteen million search results for those two words when I queried them together on Google.

And you can't argue with Google.

CHAPTER FOUR

KEEPING UP WITH THE DARWINS

My wife has a thing for cheap sunglasses.

As a consumer in this particular product category, she believes that quantity is more fun than prestige. Everywhere in her orbit, cute shades are never far from hand, and she has equal affection for each and every pair (while remaining ever vigilant for the next treasure to come her way). A few years back, we treated ourselves to a vacation in Florence, Italy, a place that reminds one of how long art and commerce have cohabited, and of how delicious a tomato can really be. Strolling among the street vendors in one of its ancient piazzas one evening, she stopped to plunder a table of sunglasses lined up in gleaming rows like SUVs in a miniature mall parking lot. Ominously, many of them were both cheap and cute. I thought this might take awhile. She quickly found a pair she liked, though, tried them on, and was amused. Until, that is, she spied the Dior logo they were sporting. Suddenly, the low price became a lot less attractive. Glaring accusingly at the shifty-looking guy behind the table, she demanded, "Where did these come from?" I think she was expecting the answer to be some far-flung factory economy.

Instead, after first looking theatrically to the right and then to the left, the vendor leaned across the table and hissed, "Mafia."

Because in Italy, seemed to be his assumption, it would be a far less serious social crime to wear stolen Dior sunglasses than it would be to wear fake ones.

It's not only in Italy that you can commit a social crime when you reach for your wallet. Consumerism and social crime are companions in just about every culture, in fact, and those social crimes are usually not as simple or as easy to walk away from as the uncertain provenance of a pair of cheap sunglasses. Nor are the consequences so fleeting. We're uncomfortable with many of the things we buy, and with many of the reasons why, we suspect, we're buying them. We chafe at the idea that our possessions might undersell what we've achieved in life, and we squirm at the possibility that we're overstating those achievements by being, as they say in Texas, "all hat and no cattle." We feel guilty or fraudulent when we treat ourselves, and foolish if we paid more than we think we needed to. We think we need to condemn brands as useless embellishments yet often miss them when they aren't there. We judge the neighbour with the new Corvette and the debt we bet he incurred to buy it, but we silently think that everybody's real estate values would improve if the guy with the shabby old Jeep would leave it in his garage instead of where people can see it. All of us, at least once in awhile, fall prey to the reflex of interpreting consumption as a signal of status and have hang-ups about it when we go shopping. "Conspicuous consumption" is a phrase usually spoken with the same cadence and enthusiasm as you would say "plaque and gingivitis."

It's no wonder. An army of well-meaning eggheads has been fretting about this for a surprisingly long time.

The phrase "conspicuous consumption" is itself, in fact, more than a century old. It first appeared in a satirical but earnest economic treatise called *The Theory of the Leisure Class*, written by economist Thorstein Veblen and published in 1899. The book was the first significant modern assault on consumerism, which is amazing when you consider that the mass-produced automobile, for example, was still almost a decade in the future. Veblen's book argued that American society was increasingly consuming in order to be observed rather than to meet practical needs; that people were deliberately imitating those in social classes above their own when they did so; that this urge was an evolutionary relic, primitive and tribal in nature; and that the whole thing was inherently classist – so much so that he reckoned the ultimate statement a conspicuous consumer could make was "abstinence from productive employment." Status, he argued, was evidenced by having more while producing less. In other words, not only were people consuming in order to declare their status, they were doing so in order to declare their dominance. He saw this as an urge so powerful that people would even sacrifice their own happiness to exercise it.

Veblen even offers a point of view on why the sunglasses salesman used theft as the explanation for his low prices:

> We find things beautiful, as well as serviceable, somewhat in proportion as they are costly. With few and inconsequential exceptions, we all find a costly hand-wrought article of apparel much preferable, in point of beauty and of serviceability, to a less expensive imitation of it, however cleverly the spurious article may imitate the costly original; and what offends our sensibilities in the spurious article is not that it

falls short in form or color, or, indeed, in visual effect in any way. The offensive object may be so close an imitation as to defy any but the closest scrutiny; and yet so soon as the counterfeit is detected, its aesthetic value, and its commercial value as well, declines precipitately. Not only that, but it may be asserted with but small risk of contradiction that the aesthetic value of a detected counterfeit in dress declines somewhat in the same proportion as the counterfeit is cheaper than its original. It loses caste aesthetically because it falls to a lower pecuniary grade.

And so, before there were very many mass-produced goods to be had and before there was much of a middle class to speak of, a new currency of social status was already being proposed for the Industrial Age. That currency would no longer be noble breeding or physical prowess or even intellect. The currency of social status would now be how much nice stuff you had, and how much you paid for it.

With the twentieth century, of course, both mass-produced goods and a middle class very quickly became realities (both, ironically, enabled by the demand for all that nice stuff). There were more of us, and more of us could afford to buy more stuff. Marketing, and brands, came of age. With that, the anxiety about what consuming means only got worse. Paul Nystrom, an American academic and seminal marketing theorist, and author of the 1928 book *Economics of Fashion*, helped add two nervous new ideas to the brew. The first was that goods of all sorts had become more about fashion than function. Fashion, by Nystrom's definition, meant consuming in order to belong to an attractive and identifiable social group. The price of *not* consuming in order to belong was high. "To be out of fashion," he declared, "is, indeed, to be out of the world." The second was the uncomfortable thesis that consumption filled a void in people's lives. The purposeless, frivolous life of the modern age, he seemed to be saying, was the most fertile possible ground for marketing. Which must have taken some of the fun out of shopping for that new Model A.

So, with the Great Depression looming like some kind of biblical flood, the idea was seeded that consumption was a crutch for spiritual weakness, giving people both a sense of purpose and a community that they were somehow unable to create on their own. Timing being everything, it's no wonder that this anxiety about consumption took such deep root in our culture.

That conspicuous consumption was a vain means of social climbing, and that having nice stuff was a poor substitute for spirituality and community, isn't in question. These human frailties have inspired a lot of branded marketing in the last hundred years or so, and they still sometimes do. I'll admit to cringing a little along with everybody else during the 1999 film *Fight Club* – a film that was all about purposelessness – when the narrator flipped through catalogs and wondered: "What kind of dining set defines me as a person?" I've been known to indulge in that sort of silly inner monologue myself the odd time, over a watch, or shoes, or how big a garden tractor I can rationalize. The fact that we're uncomfortable with the way we consume, and the way we've been manipulated to consume, is neither surprising nor without reason. But while we're beating ourselves and each other up over being such suckers, we'd be wise to remember that our collective angst about consuming is based on two assumptions that don't necessarily hold true any more.

The first has to do with social hierarchy. The realities of Veblen's times simply aren't the realities of ours. His thesis was a critique of a society hidebound by an ancient and obsolete attachment to hierarchy. To him, conspicuous consumption was a vain effort to ladder climb in a society where the social structures were rigid and economic in nature. Wealth and power came from building railroads or mining for gold, not from selling blue jeans, sneakers, and soft drinks, so the opportunities to achieve social status were more finite and abstract to the average person. That put considerable hierarchical distance between the rich and the not-so-rich. Today, this is much less the case. We may be a long way from having no class system in Western society, but our social consensus now, at least, is that there shouldn't be one. I am as worthy as you are, both of us probably believe on some level that we could be rich if we really put our minds to it, and there are a lot more ways to make that happen. We're less inclined to see ourselves as helpless about our economic destinies. And now, rather than one or two impossible leaps from the bottom to the top of the social ladder, there is an almost infinite number of rungs, and a much less strict definition of what the top looks like.

The second has to do with purpose and belonging. Nystrom's premise, and the premise of a lot of marketing in the recent past, was that we need to feel part of a group in order to be legitimate in the world. Social scientists think of these groups as communities; branded marketing people call them "market segments." Either way, the belief has always been that the need to belong was tied directly to our identities. If we weren't with others like us, we were supposedly "out of the world." But we aren't consumed by that need any more, not in the same way. In fact, there is considerable evidence to suggest that we're now striving for the opposite. We need communities around us for support, safety, and love, but our identities are increasingly our own inventions, and it's individuality, not affiliation and conformity, that we want most of all. Who we are matters at least as much as which group accepts us as a member. The idea that we spend in order to belong is, if not obsolete, then certainly a gross over-simplification of life at the mall today. And, as if to help things along, the explosion of branded marketing in the last century had the unintended consequence of promoting plurality. The more choice there was, the more the urge to individualism was empowered. Although all that choice may have appealed to our vain selves, it also quietly and inexorably drained away much of the corporate world's ability to manipulate us.

These two shifts challenge us to do something that people like Veblen and Nystrom would have thought preposterous: sep-arate the way we think about marketing and the urge to con-sume from the way we think about the idea of brands. Of course, brands have always exploited the cultural phenomenon of striv-ing and loudly cheered it on. Branded marketing has never had any motive to discourage the buying of status and affiliation or, for that matter, just being greedy – there was good money in it. Yet the mere existence of a brand generally doesn't cause this vanity in us. When a corporation gives a product a name and invests money to make that name famous, it doesn't automati-cally send us into paroxysms of soulless avarice and neurotic pining. All it does is give us leverage. After that, how we decide to react emotionally is pretty much up to us. For the consumer republic to be a possibility, we have to distinguish between what brands represent and what brands do. What brands sometimes do is create dissatisfaction, as Charles Kettering said. That's the bathwater. What they *are* is accountability. That's the baby.

So go ahead and hate marketing, if you want, but don't hate brands. That is, of course, unless they're counterfeit. That would be a crime.

———

Nothing complicates our relationship with brands more than our collection of hang-ups about their social meaning. Social meaning, as I suggested earlier, is one of the things that makes brands useful to consumers, but our hang-ups about it can blind us to the point where, sometimes, we have no capacity – or courage – for objectivity. What I've tried to persuade you in the first part of this chapter is that some of our hang-ups about brands are actually hang*overs*. They don't have a real basis any more, and they deserve to be challenged. Now, I want to persuade you that our mindsets about the social meaning of brands can actually be destructive.

For some years, I worked with Toyota. As you can imagine, this was an important assignment for the company that employed me. Toyota's marketing budget was huge, and their product line had grown to the point where it offered something for nearly everybody, from pickup trucks to minivans to sedans to, at the time, even sports cars. With so many vehicles to sell to so many different consumer target groups, an increasingly large part of our job was to figure out how to deploy that marketing budget to the greatest effect, both in terms of sales volume and of profit. Mistakes here usually had seven-figure price tags. So, for this, we needed research – not just a bunch of touchy-feely focus groups but hard data, and lots of it.

One of my favourite resources was a giant annual survey of car buyers, conducted by a company called Maritz Research. Its big, thick red binders were packed with comforting tables of data, based on a sample of thousands of new car buyers who were asked a long list of questions, including why they had chosen the car they had. And each year, when the big box of red binders arrived, we would pause from our labours and gather together in my office to mock the people who bought Porsches. Why? One question in the survey asked new owners to rank more than two dozen attributes of their new car in order of the influence each one had over their purchase decision. What was it about the car that influenced you most to buy it? What influenced you least? The attributes ranged from durability and reliability, to safety and fuel economy, to comfort and prestige. And, year after year, the majority of Porsche owners said that prestige was very low on their list of reasons for choosing that particular car. Low, as in at or near the bottom. Lower than fuel economy, for Pete's sake. Typical, we'd snort. These desperate, middle-aged guys are so insecure that they can't even be honest with a market researcher.

Indeed, in the annals of branded marketing, there is no consumer brand people love to hate more than Porsche, at least from a cultural perspective. Even today, if we were in that vacuum cleaner focus group from Chapter 2, and the moderator pensively asked (as they are wont to do), "If this vacuum cleaner were a car, what sort of car would it be?" we would reserve the answer "Porsche" for the one that cost the most, had the snobbiest image, and belonged to the owner whose house we would most like to cover in toilet paper. The stereotype is so strong that the name alone can save a Hollywood scriptwriter pages of dialogue if he wants to establish a character as a self-absorbed jerk. It is not a coincidence, for example, that Arnie Becker, the divorce lawyer in the 1980s television series *L.A. Law* and one of the biggest jerks in prime-time television, drove a white Porsche 911 Turbo. We knew who he was the minute the iconic shape of that car entered the frame. Porsches are jerkmobiles.

But what if we take the "jerk" out of the "mobile"? Objectively speaking, what does that German car company and its products offer us as justification for our derision? Not very much, as it turns out. The history of Porsche AG suggests that people with a passion for cars have had a stronger cultural influence inside that company over the years than in most larger car companies – sometimes even to its financial detriment – so they're at least relatively sincere about what they make. The majority of their vehicles are built in the most stringently regulated automobile manufacturing market on earth, in terms of the environmental impact of both the process and the vehicles themselves. According to European Union law, for example, a large percentage of the content of each car must be recycled in the home market (85 per cent, by 2015), and manufacturers have to support that process by designing material recovery right into the way their vehicles are built. Though a sports car is hardly an exemplar of environmental restraint, Porsche's manufacturing philosophy has tended to favour light weight over big horsepower to make them perform, which has some salutary environmental and fuel use benefits. Moreover, about two-thirds of the Porsches ever built are still being driven, and every one of them occupies space in garages and on roads that might otherwise be occupied by new cars, with all the new steel, rubber, plastic, and glass that implies. It's not even that hard to keep them on the road, either, given that parts are reasonably easy to find for editions dating back to the 1950s. Whether you believe that this longevity is because Porsches are well engineered or just better cared for because they're pretty, it's no small thing. The impacts of manufacturing cost and service life are so significant on the lifetime fuel cost of a vehicle that one controversial study even suggested that a Jeep Wrangler driver would eventually cost the planet less than a third as much energy as the Toyota Prius driver. Cars that last are often greener than cars that don't, almost regardless of fuel economy, and Porsches last.

Which brings us back to those poor, misunderstood Porsche drivers in the Maritz study, the ones who claimed that prestige didn't matter to them as much as reliability or safety. On reflection it turns out they might not have been lying after all. When you think about the other cars that would have been on *their* particular shopping list, their answers begin to make sense. If the other car you were considering was, say, a Ferrari of the time, then that Porsche 911 seemed all but Amish in its modest practicality by comparison.

So, do jerks drive Porsches? Probably, I guess, though I won't venture whether Porsche has the market cornered on them. But Porsche didn't make the jerks – Porsche made the cars. The social meaning of this brand is so overwhelmingly powerful and universal that nobody other than someone who already lusts for one of these cars has any motive to look past it. I don't expect you to feel bad for Porsche or the owners of their cars, nor do I think it's necessarily wise to rush out and buy one. What I want you to see is a glaring example of how social meaning, taken to extremes and without the ballast of common sense, can destroy the usefulness of brands and make us into stupid consumers. The same risk of blinding social prejudice would be present if we were talking about Hyundais or Crocs or Budweiser. Social meaning is one of the most useful things about brands. It gives consumers great leverage over corporations, until that social meaning detaches itself entirely from the product experience and becomes a cultural liability. Then, it's a problem. Then, brands don't do us any good at all.

———

"[The counterfeit] loses caste aesthetically because it falls to a lower pecuniary grade," wrote Mr. Veblen. In other words, the more we pay for something, the lovelier it seems.

If there's one aspect of conspicuous consumption we've been pretty good at renouncing over the past century or so, it's the idea that spending more makes you happier. We've fallen madly in love with cheapness (as opposed to, say, self-restraint), and in doing so have probably put our whole system of commerce in more peril than we can imagine. This is my final, and in some ways most important, argument for why we should care about brands: because, if we force them to, brands can insure us – you, me, the economy, the planet – against the scourge of cheapness.

Trained by the big manufacturing economies of the late twentieth century, most people believe that the lower a product's price, the greater the demand for that product will be, and the more of them a company will sell. Selling more stuff means that the company's production costs will fall for each piece, and its products will become both cheaper to buy and ultimately more profitable to make. Therefore, a lower price is better than a higher price, and companies that reduce prices are better than companies that do not. Meanwhile, anybody who pays more than they have to is both a fool and an accomplice in screwing up the system, and any company that charges more than it needs to is a thief. But is that really how it works? Not always. There are certainly huge companies that produce things in vast quantities, yet are somehow not profitable, or whose products aren't the cheapest, or both. One of them – General Motors – has only recently crawled out of bankruptcy at this writing. And there are certainly consumers who shopped aggressively for things on the basis of price, yet who, in the final analysis, ended up spending more instead of less than they needed to and felt ripped off about it. No, the monotheism of low price as the way to a healthy marketplace is obviously not universal and is certainly flawed, and maybe even destructive.

I'm going to tell you two truths about cheapness that I hope will make you pause before tossing that next irresistible bargain into your shopping cart.

The first has to do with how products become cheap. Remember that the corporation is a cow. It will do whatever works to get your money rather than see another cow get it. But remember also that the corporation's single reason for being is to create value for its shareholders. Value means sustainable profit, profit that the company can predictably, systematically repeat year after year. So, if you insist on paying less for everything you buy so that you can get more stuff for your money, the cow will find a way to make it happen – so long as it doesn't involve sacrificing shareholder value. How can it do this? By cutting the cost of making its products. By automating production lines. By manufacturing in places where labour is cheaper and regulations more forgiving. By using cheaper materials, or simpler assembly techniques that mean the product costs less to make but doesn't last as long. It happens in every industry, with products ranging from grocery store tomatoes to home appliances, and it's not always a bad thing. Sometimes, this sort of cost reduction pressure produces great benefits by refining and simplifying a product, making it work better or making it accessible to wider markets. We owe the fact that most of us can afford cars to Henry Ford's focus on efficient production. And particularly with new technologies, there is certainly a period in which products become both less expensive and better. More often, though, the drive to lower cost ultimately means a drive to cheapness.

Brands moderate this drive, and the reason lies in the corporate cow's need to protect shareholder value. With a single-minded focus on selling at the lowest possible price, a corporation will eventually remove content from its products to see what matters more to us. Without a brand, the only risk a corporation takes with this strategy for cheapness is that sales might suffer in the short term. With a brand, it's also risking the reputation that makes it profitable. The more famous and trusted a brand is, the more cautiously it will approach testing our tolerance for cheapness. If those lower prices mean making an embarrassing product, a corporation with a famous, trusted brand has a lot to lose.

To illustrate this last point, let's visit our friends at Toyota one more time. Among this company's products is a compact pickup truck called the Tacoma. The little truck has been immensely popular worldwide since it was introduced in 1995. But something went wrong in the manufacturing of that first series of Tacomas. Between 1995 and 2000, Toyota somehow didn't work hard enough on rust prevention for the frames of these trucks, and as the years passed, more and more of them were coming back to dealers with holes in them, many beyond repair. So what did Toyota do? In 2008 – closing in on a decade after the last affected truck rolled off the line – they offered to buy back the irreparable specimens. At 150 per cent of their book value.

Why on earth would Toyota do this? The Tacomas weren't the first rusty vehicles anybody ever made; the proof lies quietly rotting away in junkyards, ignored by the manufacturers responsible. To me, the answer is crushingly simple: Toyota remembered its terrible struggle to overcome the reputation for shoddiness Japanese cars had in the 1960s and 1970s. It had finally earned a reputation for quality in the car business, in the process becoming the world's largest carmaker and one of its most valuable brands. It simply better served the goal of sustainable profitability for them to write a cheque to everybody with a rusty Tacoma than to pretend those rusty frames were business as usual. One hundred million dollars to protect their reputation was a bargain if it meant erasing any fear their customers might have that Toyota was backsliding. Admitting fault this way might prove they were fallible, but it would also prove they weren't cheap. Their reserves of consumer goodwill would be replenished. That would be a good thing, because it wouldn't be long before they'd need it again.

Two years later, in early 2010, Toyota became mired in a succession of product safety recalls, among the biggest in history, made worse by what some saw as an opportunistic political and media firestorm. Despite a public flogging that included an appearance by company executives before Congress and an FBI investigation, a Gallup poll at the end of February 2010 – at the height of the crisis – showed that 74 per cent of owners had unshaken confidence in Toyota. Politicians and the media had been reporting Toyota's quality problems as a catastrophic betrayal of public trust. The public, on the other hand, was more sanguine. "I still trust Toyota more than [any other car company]," wrote one owner on an Internet forum at the time. Not because he thought nothing was ever going to go wrong with his vehicle, but because he knew that Toyota understood what was at stake. He knew that making a habit of cheapness would be suicidal for the world's eighth most valuable brand. He knew that Toyota's fear would be the best warranty of all.

The second truth about cheapness that should give you pause is that it makes fools of us. Our society has turned bargain hunting into a blood sport. For every time you hear someone brag about how awesome a recent purchase is, there will be a thousand times that you hear someone brag about how little they paid for it. We attach much more social currency to our ability to hang on to our money and to squeeze more out of it than we do to our ability to identify quality in a product. That would be good, if it meant we were willing to settle for less stuff in order to have better stuff. It's bad, though, if it means we're willing to settle for worse stuff in order to have more of it. The stampeding shoppers at that Walmart in Valley Stream, New York, weren't in a frenzy because the tube socks were especially attractive that year, nor were they in a frenzy because there was a critical tube sock shortage. They were in a frenzy because tube socks were on sale. We think bargain hunters are smart, and we think connoisseurs are snobs. If we don't balance those prejudices against an objective definition of value, it can make us do stupid things when we shop.

It gets worse. Today, behavioural economists are proving at a scientific level what savvy retailers have always known, that the simple fact of discounting makes us impulsive beyond reason. We too often whip out our wallets not because we need or even want but because the opportunity in front of us appears to be limited in time or quantity. Then, once we have these bargains home, we immediately proceed to treat them with all the disrespect that cheapness deserves. In *Cheap*, an excellent and

well-documented discussion of the "discount culture" phenomenon by journalist and academic Ellen Ruppel Shell, she
describes this strange behaviour: "The less we pay for something, the less we value it and the less likely we are to take care
of it, with the result that cheaper things – even if well made –
seem to wear out and break more quickly. For most of us the
fact that we paid less than full price actually discounts in our
minds the value of what we bought." The waste in this cycle
of score-keeping consumption is practically criminal, including
not only the stuff we bought that we didn't really need, but also
the cost of replacing the junk we did need but weren't careful
enough about choosing, and the resources the planet had to
surrender to make it all.

Cheapness – not to be confused with frugality – is the
socially acceptable face of greed. Sometimes that greed is corporate, and sometimes it's us, and sometimes it's both them and
us, mindlessly competing for each other's money. Regardless of
where cheapness begins, the outcome is products that don't last,
plundering the planet and filling landfill sites with the wreckage
of our short-term thinking. Cheapness exports jobs. Cheapness
gives too much power to too few retailers. Cheapness turns
shopping into a sport. It encourages us to consume for the sake
of consuming. Cheapness discourages respect for the work of
others and, ultimately, our own. Cheapness is, indisputably,
toxic to our way of life.

Still, though we shouldn't allow price alone to determine
our choices in the marketplace, neither should we allow branding to be a licence to steal our money. A brand certainly increases
the probability that a corporation will be accountable for its
products, but not without exception, and never if we take it for
granted. It's true that if you take the brand off a product, the

gloves come off, too, and marketing becomes a bloody street fight for your money rather than the more dignified pugilism of the system at its best. But even with brands, it's still a fight for value. Though they are the most potent defence we have against cheapness, brands will never be a guarantee. The opposite of cheap can't be gullible. Brands aren't an excuse not to think when we buy; they actually demand of us that we do.

PART TWO

THE NEW BLACK

MINDFUL CONSUMERISM AND THE END OF STATUS

Welcome to the revolution. Don't worry; nobody's going to get hurt. We may soon be a little more menacing at the cash register than we used to be, but the only violence we're going to inflict will be to our own disengaged complacency.

The first step in making change is to realize that brands matter. Even though they've sometimes been the name we give to corporate manipulation of our vanity for profit, and even though we might sometimes be a little embarrassed at being suckers for that, we must face the fact that brands also give us power in the marketplace that's all but political in nature. In a free marketplace, brands mean choice, and choice puts power in the hands of the people.

As citizens in a democracy, we all understand that our power comes with responsibility. We have to inform ourselves, we have to show up on election day and vote, and we have to hold the victors to their promises. It's part of the deal. Yet what's been lacking in the discourse about consumerism has been a willingness to face that very same duty in our democratic marketplaces. Pundits scribble snarky, anti-consumerist diatribes and nail them to the cathedral doors of capitalism, providing us all with someone else to blame for its failures. We all feel better shaking our fists for a little while, but at the end of the day it's hard to put the anger to any good use. It would be very difficult and almost certainly counterproductive to just check out of the system altogether, yet we're asked to believe that the system itself is intractably corrupt and broken. The result is a moral rock and a hard place. And what do humans do when we find ourselves in places like that? We tune out. We default to the status quo, and nothing changes. Accepting that we have any power to fix what's broken would mean accepting that we helped break it, or at least that we let it happen.

So let's get this out of the way right now: As with any kind of political freedom, a real consumer republic is going to take some vigilance and some effort. It's going to take humility and honesty about what really matters to us, and it's going to take a certain amount of urge control. As a great teacher of mine is fond of bluntly putting it, "If you want something you've never had, you have to do something you've never done." What we want is a sustainable way of life. What most of us have never done is put our money where our beliefs are. In the consumer republic, we're going to do that by making three promises to ourselves every time we reach for our wallets:

Buy less. Buy better. Be heard.

This section of *Consumer Republic* is about the first two promises. It considers what life might be like if, every time we shopped, we tried to make it count for something. If we got more satisfaction out of each purchase, so much so that we'd need to make fewer of them. If we chose brands to say something, to each other and to the corporations from whom we buy things, about who we are and what we stand for, rather than about where we rank on someone else's social ladder. If, instead of accounting for the deals we scored, we accounted for the differences we made when we spent our money. If, in other words, our consumption was conspicuous because it expressed who we really are rather than merely revealed our weaknesses.

It turns out that life might not be too bad at all. It might, in fact, be very satisfying indeed. All we really need to do to get there is let go of a few things – starting with our pernicious habit of keeping score.

CHAPTER FIVE

THE MYTH OF BEST

"**W**e work to become, not to acquire."

The words belong to Elbert Hubbard, an American writer and philosopher of the Arts and Crafts movement at the beginning of the last century, but I got them from Dave, my auto mechanic, who signs off all of his e-mails this way. I think he means for it to put some philosophical weight behind the virtues of preventative maintenance. It is, in any case, thunderingly true, and makes me feel pretty noble about rotating my tires. There is something liberating about knowing that it will be a long time before I have to put my ego on the line to buy a new car.

Competition turns whatever we're doing into a game. This is no less so at the mall – or at a new car dealership – than it is in football, politics, or war. Our love of winning and our aversion to losing can fog our minds and somehow excuse us from making complicated ethical decisions. We can lose any sense of right and wrong and end up ignoring the consequences of our actions. This ethical disengagement is the story of Wall Street, for example, in the financial meltdown of 2008 and 2009, when bad mortgages ended up being securitized to look like good investments. When you get right down to the human level of that disaster, it was the way the executives who made all those stupid decisions were paid that excused them from thinking about what they were really doing. Their masters were saying, in effect, what earns you a bonus – inventing and selling those securities – is the only thing you need to worry about, girls and boys. That's how we're going to keep score. This decoupled what these investment bankers and hedge fund managers did from who they might have been as human beings, and from those overmortgaged working people who would eventually lose their homes. It made capitalism a game, and it turned the players into sociopaths.

The scary thing is, each of us has the capacity to do the same thing to ourselves. Each of us has a set of base urges, relics of evolution, that occasionally kick in and invite us to be momentary sociopaths. Most of the time, tempted by an anti-social impulse – say, road rage – we know it's wrong. Mostly, we don't act on these urges, and if we do, we feel badly about it afterward and often pay the consequences directly. Consuming is different. Out there in the big, wide world, social convention and advertising don't encourage us to cheat on our taxes, administer wedgies to parking cops, jump the subway turnstile, or make inappropriate advances to the boss's spouse. Whereas, exhortations to win at the game of shopping are everywhere we look. Often, they have to do with obvious enticements – low prices or time-limited offers. Yet just as often they have to do with bragging rights. "The organized creation of dissatisfaction" is not rooted in the idea of a constantly rising objective standard for anything. It's rooted in the deadly sin of envy.

To break this cycle of sociopathic scorekeeping, we need to

continually remind ourselves of two things. And the first is that there is no "best."

If anybody could be said to be experts in the "best" business, marketing firm J. D. Power and Associates would be a good candidate. Their contribution to the world consists of lists of products and services, ranked in order of their supposed objective goodness, statistically based on the feedback of people who recently bought them. Such lists are useful resources for shopping, and a place on them is coveted by marketers, especially those who sell health plans, vacation travel, home appliances, and other high-ticket items. Making it on to these lists is one of the ways a brand can build a reputation for quality. It's also one of their favourite ways of proving a claim to it in advertising. However, when you spend some time pondering lists like the ones that J. D. Power makes, you start to notice something about the brands that win the highest ratings. You notice, for example, that price isn't much of a predictor of "bestness." The "best" products are rarely the most expensive, nor for that matter are they the cheapest. Nor does being best line up neatly with being famous. Highly ranked brands aren't uniformly the most legendary or special in any obvious sense, nor are they obscure and specialized outliers. There is, in other words, no simple meritocracy in which better equals more expensive and more famous. The brands and their products ranked "best" often seem to be simply the ones that are the least troublesome to the most people. The objectively best products are often simply the most common.

Consider, for example, the list of refrigerators in J. D. Power's *2009 Home Appliance Study*. The "best" fridge was, in their estimation at that point in time, a Samsung. It's a very fine refrigerator, I'm sure. Still, this brand's victory is striking for two reasons. One is that Samsung is not a particularly elite brand on the face of it. It hails from a cost-efficient Asian market, and its products aren't generally super-exotic in their engineering or their prices. In fact, so common are they that Samsung refrigerators occupy close to one-fifth of the appliance showroom floor space in the United States. And the other reason that its ranking is noteworthy is that, despite its putative superiority, Samsung isn't the only company selling fridges. Somehow, the "bestness" of this product seems to have eluded a lot of appliance shoppers who are merrily buying fridges elsewhere. Or has it? Look at the list of attributes that J. D. Power has scored in the refrigerator category: "Overall satisfaction," "Ease of use," "Performance," "Styling and feel," "Features," "Warranty," and "Price." At least half of those qualities are, from one person to the next, very much in the eye of the beholder. A numeric score for any of these would not alter the fact that you as an individual might insist on a side-by-side, while I could not live without an icemaker. It's doubtful, actually, that any two people share exactly the same definition for any of these attributes, including affordability. To make matters even murkier, a quick search of product review sites on the Web reveals that even Samsung refrigerators are not without their problems, nor does every shopper's resource concur with J. D. Power's ranking. "Best" seems to depend on whom you ask.

Meditate on this list of refrigerators for a while longer, and you'll reach two more conclusions: First, most mainstream products are alike in more ways than they are different when it comes to their basic function. Those bearing a familiar brand are likely able to do what they're designed to do, and unlikely to make a fool of you for choosing them. The second conclusion you might reach is that assessments of "best" are rarely as objective as they seem. Complete objectivity is all but impossible in a world with so much stuff to choose from and so little risk of buying something that simply doesn't work. There is no best; there's only a best for you, and another for me, and a few billion others for everybody else at the mall. It's absurd to let an urge to inflict envy on others influence the way we spend our money when, at the end of the day, the guy who waves that list at us bragging that he's bought the best refrigerator has probably only bought the one the fewest people hate. That's not much to be proud of, much less to envy.

The second point we constantly need to keep in mind is that the urge to keep objective score of how smart we are at the mall can, paradoxically, make us do irrational things. The idea of coming in second is so odious to us that, in our effort to avoid it, we end up losing all sense of context, and thereby become suckers for manipulative marketing. This blindness can actually turn us into the prey we fear we are in the marketplace. Think about the way retailers conduct sales. We can all nod in recognition of that little adrenaline rush we feel when we stumble on to those 99-cent tube socks, and it's not hard to see ourselves buying them whether they were on our shopping list or not and gloating to our friends about it afterward. Everybody loves to score a deal, which does nothing to discourage the idea that shopping is a sport. But getting more for less without regard to our needs is only the most obvious way this blindness works. In fact, many of us get green-eyed at the idea that anybody we know has more horsepower, fluffier towels, better-smelling armpits, or more signal bars on their cellphones than we have. Few things make us reach for our wallets faster than being on the wrong end of comparison.

Here's an example of what I mean. Imagine that you're the Chief Marketing Officer for a big cable company. It's the end of the 1990s, and it's becoming obvious that Internet access is something that every household is going to need and buy as surely as it does electricity. Moreover, that access is getting faster and more reliable all the time, with broadband technology evolving to the point where it could be reasonably priced for the average consumer. Broadband, everybody in the marketing world knows by then, is going to be the key to doing business on-line. Up to that time, the average person's use of the Internet had been limited to e-mail and accessing static information; with high-speed access, the web could be more useful, more fun, and more absorbingly interactive than anybody has ever experienced. That would make people want it and be willing to pay for access to it. (Some wide-eyed freaks even thought people might choose the Web over television one day. Imagine.)

Cable companies, including Canada's Rogers Communications, with whom I worked at the time, saw an important opportunity, and they were not about to go the way of the railroads by missing it. They had a technology that would let them deliver high-speed Internet through wires that they already ran into millions of homes, and it could be sold and paid for in the same way their current products were. There was just one problem: Most cable companies were on the defensive with their customers. Consumers viewed them as ruthless monopolists who took full advantage of the fact that most customers had no choice but to deal with them. As a breed and despite their short history, cable companies seemed like old-school, fat-cat businesses. That's a tough platform from which to sell a bright, shiny, technology-empowered future.

So what would you do? How would you sell your new product? Well, being a rational human being, you would probably start with the advantages of the product itself, since connection speeds are objectively measurable. Faster, you might claim in your ads, is better and, for the moment, you're the fastest game in town. And that's just what most cable operators did. They ran advertisements that told people straight out how much faster a cable modem was than their dial-up connection, and let the ambient mania for the Web do the rest.

Rogers approached it a little differently. They needed this technology to redeem their brand if they were going to have a bright, shiny future of their own. Like many cable operators in North America, Rogers wasn't just in the cable business but the wireless, publishing, and broadcasting businesses, too. They had a huge stake in the coming media revolution. The marketing obstacle for them wasn't whether they could sell high-speed Internet competitively; it was whether their customers could be persuaded to trust them. How could they convince a consumer, irritated at having to pay for the Drywall Channel in order to get his MTV, to let the same cable company bring them the biggest cultural phenomenon since television itself? The answer was to change the subject and talk about *that*, and not about megabits per second. To give the connection speed pitch an irresistible emotional context. Instead of selling you the pipe, this cable company was going to make you think about all the magical things that might come through that pipe in the years ahead. The whole glorious strategy was encoded in the breathless slogan:

"You're not going to miss all this, are you?"

The campaign behind this slogan essentially wrapped the promise of superior product performance inside a rhetoric of social pressure. And it worked. In creative tests, consumers exposed to an objective product message were challenging and skeptical; consumers exposed to the "miss all this" message were excited and receptive. In the marketplace, the results delivered on that promise. Not only did Rogers sign up lots of high-speed Internet subscribers and stem the outflow of disgruntled customers to other service providers, but they also made real progress in repositioning their brand. The monopolistic old cable guys now appeared to be a competitive integrated telecommunications company. As it happened, you couldn't really go wrong by buying this particular product, but the way it was sold reveals a rather unattractive truth about the way we think. Our need to avoid being seen as losers is so great that it sometimes makes us irrational to the point of looniness. Simply put, people are far more worried by the risk of losing tangible advantage than they are excited by a gamble that might win them something. New technology is a gamble, especially if it comes from a brand you don't especially like. But missing out on *the whole freaking future*? Unacceptable. Especially if our neighbours might not be.

It gets worse. We are actually willing to suffer rather than see a peer gain an advantage over us. You read that right. If we peel back the layers of civilized convention and conditioned morality, we, as a species, are sometimes impulsive blockheads who would rather miss a meal altogether than see anybody else eat a better one than ours. Sometimes that even means parting with our money to buy things we didn't really want.

Social scientists call this "loss aversion." Nobel winner Daniel Kahneman, Richard Thaler, Dan Ariely, and other modern thinkers in the world of economics frequently refer to loss aversion as the evolutionary quirk most likely to distract people from making rational decisions, about anything from love to weed whackers. This sad state of affairs isn't even all that modern. Apparently, we've been blockheads since at least the mid-eighteenth century. Adam Smith, the Scottish moral philosopher, a father of economics and author of the seminal *The*

Wealth of Nations, wrote, in 1759, "We suffer more . . . when we fall from a better to a worse situation, than we ever enjoy when we rise from a worse to a better." This seems to hold true not only when there is some kind of actual loss, but also in cases when our *relative* status changes. We can think we have the best weed whacker in the neighbourhood until our neighbours buy newer ones. Then, suddenly, we have the fourteenth best weed whacker in the neighbourhood, and the same garden implement that made us so happy last week is now a painful reminder of our inadequacy. This quirk of ours is what makes us such suckers for any sales pitch that implies someone else might end up better off than we are if we don't do something about it. We roar off to the mall to make things right, without a single thought to whether our lawns are going to look any different next week than they did last. It's crazy.

Consuming can be many things but a competitive sport should never be one of them. When we keep score of our performance as consumers, we're caught between the impossibility of objective measurement and the blinding urge to win at something. Shopping becomes a mindless, compulsive, wasteful, and empty experience. Our own competitiveness makes us hate marketing even as it makes us more susceptible to its rhetoric, and that in turn lets the wrong kind of marketing succeed. Meanwhile, every dollar we spend playing the game is another opportunity lost to make our money count for something.

Dante was right about the perils of envy. And Dave is right about preventative automobile maintenance. The money we make for the work we do in life has more noble purposes than to keep score for the world to see. We should spend to become, not to acquire.

And we should absolutely rotate our tires.

———

The need to win isn't the only way "bestness" affects the way we shop. Toss a little insecurity into the mix and things get even more interesting. The prize of social acceptance can be just as intoxicating as victory, and the pursuit of it can make us just as crazy.

Most people remember high school society as ruthless and totalitarian. It certainly was for me, and maybe even a little more for me than for some. You see, I went to a country school in a part of the world where ideological pluralism was confined to the realm of pickup trucks. Chevy, Dodge, and Ford owners rose above their differences to coexist in tense peace. Beyond that, full participation in the community had more to do with what people had in common and, being Canadian, civility depended on keeping one's differences to oneself. In my high school, though, no such civil convention existed. What made you different may not have been declared by you, but it definitely was observed. By a mob. And the taxonomy was pretty simple: you were cool, or you were not.

You couldn't buy status, either, though that didn't stop kids like me from trying. Every few years, some item of clothing or recreational gear would come along that aroused a mania among the annointed cool kids and, in the rest of us, a momentary sense of possibility that the tribe could be joined for a price. If you could manage to pump enough gas or mow enough lawns, a pair of Levi's jeans was the first totem you acquired in your quest for acceptance. In those days, Levi's cost a little more money, and then as now were tailored more for style than work. Thus, in a rural community, Levi's carried none of the agricultural undertones of brands like Wrangler or GWG. If you wore

Levi's to school, it removed any doubt about your sartorial intentions. You were rebel chic. Rather than being on your way to or from the barn, you were clearly, as Veblen put it, "[abstaining] from productive employment." Still, make no mistake, you had to be able to pull it off. Levi's did not confer status in and of themselves but rather were an *emblem* of status, and the cool kids policed and protected the social meaning of that emblem with ruthless, totalitarian efficiency. If you showed up at school one morning wearing pants that were above your caste, you wouldn't even make it to lunch hour before one of them would sneak up behind you and rip off the little orange Levi's tab on the right rear pocket of your new jeans. This simple act of vandalism would render your jeans utterly, abjectly anonymous, return you socially from whence you had come, and leave you with a badge of shame that, depending on your rate of growth, could last the rest of the academic year. You were either one of them, or you weren't. It wasn't negotiable.

The need to identify with a group is a potent human drive. Most of us don't want to feel alone in the world, even if we think we want to be unique. The oft-cited Abraham Maslow, whom you'll recall from the Introduction, even reckoned that external validation by one's social group was a fundamental "esteem" or "belonging" need, the last stage before self-actualization in his hierarchy of needs. Needs, though, however universal, can be dangerous, both in life and at the mall. Wherever you find a need, you will also find power conferred on whomever is able to meet it, power that means that need might only be met at a cost. If that need is for validation by a group, the price might be conformity. Conformity, as it happens, has something in common with many of the deals we consumers sign up for: the hidden costs can be forehead-slappingly high.

Liz Suhay is an Assistant Professor in the Department of Government and Law at Lafayette College in Easton, Pennsylvania, where she studies and teaches political psychology. She arrived there from the University of Michigan in 2008 with a freshly minted Ph.D. behind her name and a dissertation under her arm entitled *Group Influence and American Ideals: How Social Identity and Emotion Shape Our Political Values and Attitudes*. The question it proposed to answer was disarmingly simple: Why does social influence occur? Since the dawn of time, nobody who studies the human condition has ever doubted that social influence is all around us and critical to getting anything done, but surprisingly few academics had ever tried to dissect the mechanics of it. Most of those who had, Suhay wrote, "typically attribute influence to persuasion, i.e., to argumentation and information exchange." She believes it's not so simple, or so rational. Suhay cites the work of experimental psychologists who have proven that "social influence often occurs in *the absence* [italics hers] of meaningful information exchange or logical argument. In other words, individuals often mold their views to those of their peers after simply learning peers' beliefs or preferences, nothing more."

Suhay calls her explanation for "group pressure" the Social-Emotional Influence (SEI) Theory, and it's compelling in its intuitive logic. First, it reveals that we're more than a little complicit in the phenomenon of peer pressure. Groups influence our choices not by force but by invitation. Why? Because the only groups that have the power to influence us are those that we have, in effect, decided we want to identify with. Second, the nature of the influence can be overwhelmingly emotional. Long before – or even without – receiving information from a group, or even before understanding its biases, we're prone to feeling pride when we're aligned with it and shame when we're not. Third, the compulsion to feel as little shame and as much pride as possible is so strong that it can make us ignore not just information but even our own values, if they're in conflict with that alignment. Simply put, we're capable of forgetting ourselves simply in order to belong. We don't all succumb to this all the time, she says, but we're all vulnerable to it. When a prominent doctor of a different sort, of a generation previous to Liz Suhay's work, posed the question, "I'm a Pepper, he's a Pepper, she's a Pepper, we're a Pepper, wouldn't you like to be a Pepper, too?" the answer might very well have been yes, if the other Peppers hadn't been so hopelessly lame.

Suhay applied her concept of SEI to the study of citizenship rather than consumerism. She is quick to acknowledge, however, that the phenomenon almost inevitably occurs in consumer culture as well, and that it's no trivial thing. That's because we'll not only comply with a group consensus, we'll find a way to really believe in it, too. "We actually come to like [products we buy] more, due to social influence," she told me. "And the pride we feel is psychologically 'stamped' on the object." So, by the way, is the shame of non-compliance. This "stamping" process is at work in the way that people respond to all kinds of popular culture (and the creators of that culture, in fact, aggressively seek it out). It also drives the way we behave in focus groups, on Internet message boards and in Facebook groups, and in the coffee klatsch while our kids are at soccer practice. And it is the obsession of Madison Avenue. There is no higher prize in marketing than to create a "stamp" like this and to succeed in building consensus around it in a marketplace. It's what every ad campaign has ever hoped to do. It's what every cow hopes its brand will become.

Whether a group is ad hoc, focused on a single issue, virtual or real, the need for external validation, the need to reflect and be a reflection of some kind of community ideal, seems to influence our behaviour as consumers almost every day of our lives. I didn't use to think there was anything dangerously wrong with that and I mostly still don't. Yet it's sobering to know that this need can be so blinding. It's one thing to seek approval – that sort of human frailty is harmless most of the time – but to be willing to both turn off our brains and forget who we are in order to get that approval is just as unnerving in its implications for a consumer republic as it is for a political one. It means that we could be filling our homes with expensive mistakes as surely as we sometimes fill the halls of government with the same thing. It means we could be wasting our money on stuff that's meant to impress people who probably haven't paid any attention to us since high school, people who, as my mom used to say, aren't worth impressing in the first place. It means we could be spending our hard-earned money (or, worse, taxing our credit limits) and plundering the planet to acquire things that in the long run will mean precisely nothing to us.

I can't think of a worse kind of consumerism than that. At any price.

＊

———

Do you have favourite things? Are there objects in your life that you actually care about, that you have some kind of irrational attachment to? For most of us there are and, more often than we might care to think, those favourite things started out as consumer products. In my case, it's mostly the usual guy stuff. A watch I had no business buying but is now the only one I wear and will be passed down to my son someday. A guitar I bought in college. A decade-old sports car, improved upon by its manufacturer many times over since mine was built but which fits me like an old catcher's mitt. An English trench coat from the '80s – hopelessly out of fashion now, yet so sturdily made and well travelled that I hang on to it just in case fashion favours me one more time. Unless we're monk-like ascetics or shallow beyond belief, we all have a few possessions we bought years ago that have stuck with us along life's road longer than we thought they would. These talismans have three things in common: They are few in number. They aren't, by design, cheap or disposable. And they are personal. When we chose them, for one brief moment, we weren't thinking about anybody's approval but our own.

People are competitive beasts by nature just as corporations are, and for the same underlying reason, rooted in the distant past: winners live, and losers perish. The weak were once culled from the gene pool, and the strong had their aggression reinforced by winning prizes – shelter, a good breeding partner, a nice hunk of fresh mastodon. In corporate life, this compete-or-die dynamic remains valid some of the time, although I think it's also too often used as an excuse for destructive marketing, the kind of marketing that draws out our own worst urges, and, in turn, encourages the scoundrels. The truth is that what we choose to put in our shopping carts is not a matter of life and death. Back on our suburban culs de sac, what we bring home from the mall is not going to cause us to be cast out into the wilderness or, for that matter, crowned head of the tribe. The reflexive obsession with comparison – whether it's to feel superior, to avoid being disadvantaged, or simply to gain acceptance – is a useless evolutionary vestige. It is, in this sense, a bit like armpit hair.

No, from the sages of ancient Greece to the seer Oprah, philosophers of every age and stripe agree vigorously that the essential precondition to happiness in this life is to "know thyself." This timeless aphorism is said to have been inscribed on the wall of Apollo's temple at Delphi (along with "nothing in excess," about which more later). It even turns up in *The Matrix*, so you know it has to be profound. Along with being a sound philosophical starting point for personal growth, spiritual evolution, and a life well lived, it's also, I believe, a good starting point for deciding how to spend our money. Show me a case of buyer's remorse, and I'll show you someone who fell prey to at least one of the primitive urges I've laid bare in this chapter. That remorseful consumer let vanity, or greed, or the fear of being left out prod him into reaching for his wallet; he tried to win. Whereas, show me a product that someone has owned for a very long time, one its owner still finds satisfying to use and happily calls "mine," and I will show you a consumer who spends her money on the basis of how a purchase will improve her life, rather than her image, or else doesn't spend it at all. The dumps and garage sales of the nation are full of last year's cellphones and moon boots. What you will rarely find in either of those places is an object someone once cherished as his or her favourite.

Without a doubt, applying the "favourite" standard is going to make shopping harder work. For a start, when we buy a product, we're going to have to ponder rather than pounce. We'll need to think not just about the day we bring our new widget home but about the years that will follow. We're going to have to imagine ourselves using it as opposed to just having it, and imagine it fitting into our lives. We're going to have to choose that widget as if it were the last one we'll ever own. We'll start to see "good enough" or "it'll do for now" as an ugly prelude to a misdemeanour against humanity. That, in turn, means we're going to come home from the mall empty-handed once in awhile, and sometimes we won't make the trip at all. Finally, we're going to have to be steadfast about our choices, because there's always the chance that our blockhead friends will give us a hard time for wasting our money or missing out on something.

But if we can set this standard for the way we buy, two magical things will happen.

The first is obvious. As time goes by, we'll find ourselves deriving so much more satisfaction out of the things we spend our money on that we'll feel the need to buy less often and less compulsively and to replace them less frequently. Inevitably, we will one day be able to look around us in every direction and see nothing but possessions that were worth working for. There will be no junk. Every material item of any significance in our lives will be something that we conscientiously chose; something that provided utility or beauty, and did so on our terms; something that made us feel good about our judgment and our priorities, and respected the effort it took to afford it.

The second is less obvious, but even more important. The signal that this kind of consumerism will send to the corporate world will be powerful and transformational. For one thing, cash registers will ring less often, so marketers won't be able to take consumers for granted any more. They will value our purchase occasions and fight hard for them, rather than think of them as inexhaustible. For another, they will start to care very deeply about the integrity of their brands, because the short memory that goes with mindless consumption will be a thing of the past. Investing more of ourselves in how we buy, and having higher expectations when we do, will make short work of brands that don't keep their promises. Finally, products might just get better, which is infinitely preferable to the ephemeral, chest-thumping "best." Corporations might start to think about how well they could make their products rather than about how cheaply, which all by itself would be world-changing. This kind of consumerism would change what corporations have to do to survive, and very much for the better.

Indeed, the people corporations rely on to tell them what's on our minds are already sounding the alarm. Yankelovich, Inc. is one of the most trusted and respected market research companies in the world. In a November 2009 report entitled *A Darwinian Gale: The Recovery Consumer Marketplace in the Era of Consequences*, they warned marketers in no uncertain terms:

> In the redefinition of value in the recovery consumer marketplace, prioritization will replace accumulation as the defining passion of consumption . . . The necessity to prioritize will demand greater attention and deliberation, thus elevating rational elements in consumer decision-making. Emotions won't become unimportant, far from it. But forced to think more about what they buy, and [empowered by] new ways of getting input and feedback, consumers will be exceptionally attentive to rational, deliberative factors. Many habits deeply ingrained and long practiced without thinking will be rethought, then reset. . . . With [this] will come some scaling down. In developed economies, the mass market will lose much of its affinity with the lifestyles of the super-rich.

In other words, the handwriting is already on the wall. We're going to buy less rather than just pay less, and we're going to make sure it counts when we do. The rules are about to change, Yankelovich is telling the corporate herd, and you cows had better be ready.

The myth of "best," of course, is that consumerism is a game to be won. Money, that almighty proxy for what we've accomplished in life, can only be observed when it's converted into stuff. So, in order to make sure that everybody can take the measure of our life's work, we create this lingua franca of accumulation. We collect points by having the best stuff and getting the best deals, and by filling our closets, cupboards, and garages with the dust-collecting trophies. Yet we know "best" is a mirage. Whether it's sold to us as a marketing promise or imposed on us by social influence, the idea of "best" is like those mechanical rabbits that make greyhounds run faster. We'll never catch it, and we wouldn't enjoy it much if we did. Nothing good comes of keeping score. In the end, all it does is absolve everyone – marketers and consumers alike – from having to think about the consequences of what they are doing. And that's a luxury none of us can afford.

Consuming can't be a game any more; of that there can be no doubt. The question is, what should it be? I've got an answer that might surprise you, and it begins, coincidentally, just down the hall from the mastodons.

CHAPTER SIX

A HORIZONTAL CLASS SYSTEM

If there were an Indiana Jones of free market consumerism, that person would be Grant McCracken, Ph.D.

On his blog, McCracken describes himself as an anthropologist and ethnographer, but this dry characterization gives short shrift to a fascinating career path. Although most people think of cultural anthropology as the study of extinct or exotic societies, McCracken has been, from the beginning of his career, much more interested in the one we're living in right now, and in "the interactions of culture and commerce" that reveal its nature. His jungle is the mall, and his sacred runes are ads and brands. He has written several books on this and related subjects, has taught at the University of Cambridge (anthropology), MIT (ethnography), and Harvard Business School (marketing), and has consulted to brands such as Coca Cola, IBM, IKEA, and Chrysler. He is a smart guy, and the fact that he has chosen to practise his craft by studying a culture that is still unfolding at a million miles an hour makes him an academic swashbuckler.

We met in 1993 when I was working with a firm that had won a government agency contract to develop an anti-smoking advertising campaign directed at young teens. A colleague of mine who had been a student of McCracken's invited him to help us, and for a stupendously good reason: McCracken had recently finished mounting an exhibit on youth cultures at the Royal Ontario Museum (ROM) – home to the aforementioned mastodon, among other ossified species. The exhibit was called Toronto Teenagers: Coming of Age in the 1990s. At that moment, nobody else within our grasp knew more about contemporary teen life than he did, so it made perfect sense to ask his help. His contribution to that project was invaluable, and the initiative was very successful. What stuck with me through all the years since then, though, was his show at the ROM. There, among the towering posed skeletal remains of extinct predators and prey, I think I saw the future of conspicuous consumption.

In the work that led to the ROM exhibit, Grant McCracken had embarked on a simple scientific inquiry: to study youth in a major metropolitan centre, using the perspective and analytical tools of cultural anthropology. Put simply, if kids were a lost tribe living in an exotic foreign land and he were to wade ashore and observe them to figure out what made their society tick, what would he find? The surprising answer was that urban youth weren't a single tribe at all. Using the familiar cultural cues that help a social scientist define a society – customs and mores, language, music and art, mode of dress – McCracken found *fifteen* distinct social groups of teenagers roaming the streets of Toronto waiting for their lives to happen. Just as surprising, to me at least, was that these tribes weren't castes. They weren't a hierarchy, a series of rungs on a social ladder. Rather, they were part of a pluralistic larger society in which what made you different was of greater cultural importance than what made you the same. And each tribe was as distinct in its worldview as it was in its style. As McCracken put it, "We [were] not just talking about lots of differences. We were talking about differences with depth . . . differences of fashion, clothing – the differences of the surface – turned out to indicate differences below. Differences of values and perspective." In other words, maybe for the first time ever, looking at a teenager didn't tell you where they ranked in a social pecking order, it told you who they were.

Today these kids are in their thirties, full-blown consumers with careers and families and homes and cars in their driveways. With growing households, a little disposable income for the first time in their adult lives, and not many birthdays away from their peak earning years, they are, for marketers, a demographic sweet spot. As we ask ourselves what modern consumerism could be, I can't help but wonder if somewhere inside their adult selves they've managed to preserve their adolescent approach to culture and consumption. Because, if they have, they might just hold the key to freedom from the tyranny of status. Those teenagers, you see, were doing two things that their predecessors had never done, and that Madison Avenue never anticipated in the days of *The Hidden Persuaders*.

The first has to do with plurality. Because their society was a constellation of tribes rather than a caste system, the tribe each teen belonged to was, to a large extent, a matter of choice. Undoubtedly, conditions and costs existed for entry to each one. You probably couldn't just wake up one day, decide to be a Goth, buy some black clothes, and be immediately welcomed into that group, but at least these kids had some degree of autonomy in the matter. In generations past, your social fate as a teenager was determined by where you lived, what your father did for a living, how wealthy your family was or wasn't, and whether you were handy with a stick and ball or a skipping rope. The groups were many fewer in number and your affiliation was initially, at least, thrust upon you and determined your status. Walking through the exhibit at the Royal Ontario Museum, though, one had the impression that the youth of the last decade of the twentieth century perceived their world as a buffet. The imperative was choice, not conformity. Rather than simply fighting their way toward adulthood, they were fighting their way toward individuality.

The second has to do with those "cultural cues" I mentioned earlier. In McCracken's work with us on teen smoking cessation, he identified that the real challenge was not one of being persuasive, but of being relevant. Teens, he observed, are deeply engaged in constructing a "self." (It was in this context that smoking held such power for some of them, and the reason they'd been so immune to rational argument: the possibility of premature death decades in the future couldn't compete with the attraction of the immediate entry smoking provided into a supportive tribe.) Inventing an adult self has always been the work of adolescents, of course. In the past, though, building this self was a little like growing into a hand-me-down suit. You were supposed to fill it, not create it. Whereas what attracted the attention of these modern teens – what was useful to them – were opportunities to autonomously declare themselves. Rather than just aligning themselves with a group, they were interested in making observable choices that would explain who they were to their peers. These choices would also, along the way, help them assemble an identity they could authentically call their own. And many of these choices involved acts of consumption. For every tribal custom and bit of slang to emerge organically in each of these tribes, there was also inevitably a hat, a pair of sneakers, a recording artist, or a piece of recreational gear that spoke for the chooser, within his or her group, as well as to society at large. Choice gave the youth of the 1990s the luxury of creating, as McCracken called it, a "custom-built [self]." That building process happened partly in the marketplace, and may have provided the first autonomous consumer experiences some of these kids had ever had. That means, for a lot of them, at a time in their lives when not much of their autonomous spending was likely to have been on groceries and car payments, consuming was a purely creative act. In the 1990s, for a sixteen-year-old with any money to spend, no purchase was mindless. Everything meant something. Consuming wasn't about acquiring, it was about curating.

A creative act. Think about that for a minute. Sure, teenagers of any generation are rarely exemplary consumers. Half of what they buy is ephemeral by nature, and the other half is too small for them in six months. But in this one sense, the young consumers of Generation X were geniuses. Their tribal choices, even once made, remained fluid and provisional. They would drift in and out of the groups they chose to belong to, create individual interpretations of the ethos of those groups, and find a thousand ways to make sure that observers knew that while they might be *in* a particular place, they were never going to be *of* that particular place. This wariness of conformity extended directly to consuming, which they did not only with creativity but also with a subversive purpose when it came to brands. Douglas Rushkoff captured the feistiness of it all this way: "In conscious defiance of demographic-based pandering, [youth] adopt a stance of self-protective irony – distancing themselves from the emotional ploys of the advertisers." At the time, it may simply have seemed like a sophisticated kind of adolescent rebellion. Today, though rebellion may not figure much into the lives of those thirtysomething former culture jammers, I think their legacy is still with us. They rediscovered the soul of consumerism, its most noble purpose: the tearing down of class structures through defiant self-expression. The Baby Boomers gave us rock and roll. Generation X gave us cultural autonomy.

Though you wouldn't know it sometimes. The bill of goods sold to us by activists, academics, and journalists of one stripe or another is that marketing promotes status anxiety, and that this is what makes us chomp our way through the mall like Pac Man. This simplistic view is helpfully reinforced by entertainment media, who find class stereotypes an efficient storytelling tool. And, okay, yes, there are still some idiotic marketers out there who cling desperately to the same fairy tale. So maybe we think we should still believe it. Maybe all this does perpetuate the concept of status, and maybe we still genuinely have pangs of it now and then. But if status anxiety is still a theme in modern life, it's almost certainly little more than an evolutionary vestige of a simpler society from a long-gone past. We just don't roll that way any more. In a white paper on upcoming 2010 U.S. Census data, written for the marketing trade publication *Ad Age*, demographer Peter Franchese called it like this: "The concept of an 'average American' is gone, probably forever . . . The average American has been replaced by a complex, multidimensional society that defies simplistic labeling." Indeed, when the Census Bureau sent out its survey in the spring of 2010, it had to offer Americans no fewer than fourteen choices to describe just their family relationships. "Typical," even a government has to admit, is a thing of the past in North America. The social plurality of young people a generation ago has become the plurality of our entire culture.

That means that conspicuous consumption has been turned utterly sideways. Make no mistake, consumption is always going to be conspicuous, even if we're reduced to wearing bearskins. But if there are no herds we're forced to join, if there is no status ladder to be climbed, if there is no majority sitting in judgment of our choices, then why, beyond meeting our basic needs, do we buy the things we do? Whom are we trying to impress? The answer those kids offered us, there among the mastodons, was that we buy to be, not to belong. That if we are going to invest our money – the dividend of the work we spend half our lives doing – in anything beyond what we need, we should make doing it a creative act. We should curate the things we surround ourselves with so that they speak for us rather than give us a uniform to hide behind. Those teenagers, deeply engaged in the work of defining themselves and having limited resources to work with, simply couldn't afford the luxury of unexamined consumption.

The best news is, they walk among us still.

———

You see a lot of black clothing in advertising agencies. Black jeans, black tee-shirts, black skirts, black raincoats, black sneakers, black sweaters, and for that matter probably (though I can't confirm this) black underwear. Design companies, too. Anybody in the branding business, really. Even people who teach it in universities. Clichéd as it is, black is still the colour of choice for creative professionals whose job it is to make brands meaningful and attractive to us. Some of the younger ones are getting cleverer about it, resorting instead to pointedly bland American Apparel or something hiply obscure like Muji. But the objective is the same: semiotic opacity. They don't want to be figured out. Charitably, maybe, they want to present an agnostic face in their professional environment, the better to be trusted by their peers and clients. Less charitably, maybe, they want to seem somehow above what they do. Advertising people can be like that sometimes. Plagued with self-doubt and guilt about the supposed problem they're getting paid to create, perhaps they wear the same clothes every day as penance for getting everybody into this pickle, like the Skipper on *Gilligan's Island*.

While I was working on *Consumer Republic*, a colleague sent me the URL for a blog that looked intriguing. It was called "5brand" and it appeared to be a kind of independent social experiment in the cultural meaning of brands. Visitors to the site were challenged to answer one simple question: "Could you define yourself with only 5 brands?" The best part of the original site (at this writing, the creators are moving from the Tumblr blogging platform to a site of their own) was that you could see how other people had answered the question.

Not surprisingly, I found 5brand fascinating. The famous brands you would expect to be on everybody's list (Apple or Starbucks, for example) often were. However, countless obscure brands not only added depth to the profiles of the people who had responded, they also made them look more interesting. Sometimes people associated a brand with something they did professionally or recreationally, and sometimes they identified with the ethos of a brand whether they were consumers of it or not. But the most surprising thing about 5brand was who responded to the challenge. In the first few months of the experiment, the vast majority of those who contributed answers were actually *in the branding business* – designers, art directors, strategic planners, media people, the whole menagerie. And they came from all over the world. It turns out, based on this very small, very unscientific sample, that all those guilty-looking people in black actually have a great deal to say about themselves, and the symbolic language they choose to say it in is the one they have in common and speak most fluently: brands.

The creators of 5brand, in fact, don't toil in the parched vineyards of Madison Avenue where a lot of the brands you see on their site were born. Founder Alessandro Jacoby and his colleagues are from emergent Brazil, where Jacoby divides his time between teaching and creative directing at an advertising agency. 5brand is, he told me, "an exercise in self-awareness through brands," and is ultimately "not about brands, but about perception." This is what is perhaps most interesting of all to me about 5brand. It seems to be completely irony-free. North Americans are so suspicious of branded marketing that they wouldn't admit to identifying with it on a bet, even as they stood defiantly in their Pumas. But take that sense of wariness out of the equation, either by being in the branding business or by working in a market whose culture is less easily threatened by branded marketing, and the cultural utility of brands is revealed.

The argument that *Consumer Republic* makes is that we can make consumption more sustainable if we make it more mindful. If we invest more of ourselves in what we buy, we might buy less stuff and do it much more carefully. Jacoby's experiment suggests that brands are a language we could use to do that. So could all those black turtlenecked carpetbaggers be on to something? Do we all, indeed, possess some fluency in the cultural language of brands? And would speaking it more often make us into better consumers?

The first question is easy. We are absolutely fluent in the cultural language of brands. When market researchers talk with consumers about almost anything, from a political candidate to a condo development, they will often resort to brand analogies to do it. And not just poor old Porsche. Most people are able to use countless famous brand names easily – and with great precision – as cultural code. Few comparatives give a researcher deeper or more nuanced results than asking people to paint a portrait of something or someone using only brands as the colours. When it comes to analogies, it's the biggest, richest, most broadly understood language there is, unless you happen to hang around with botanists. If I asked you to characterize your spouse as an alcoholic beverage, you could probably do it with ease. Your employer as a fast-food chain, your bank as a technology company, your city as a pair of sneakers – it's a game people are almost eager to play, and we're all very, very good at it. (Champagne, Taco Bell, Microsoft, and New Balance, in case you were wondering.) Brands are spoken here.

The best way to answer the second question – would speaking that language more often make us into better consumers? – is, ironically, an analogy. Imagine that we were not talking about consumer goods, but about food. Let's suppose that you've decided you're going to eat more carefully. For you, this isn't a matter of dieting – which is punitive, generally temporary and remedial – but of actually paying attention to every single morsel you put in your body. How would your way of life change? You'd eat less, that's almost certain. But in doing that, you'd probably also make a point of eating better. You might decide to go the slow food route, or perhaps the 100-mile one, or maybe even grow some of your own food. Your inspirations might be Mediterranean, or Asian, or maybe the work of some great chef; they will, in any case, be personal choices. Regardless of your strategy, you would make eating a mindful pursuit rather than a compulsive one. You would focus on extracting as much pleasure from the act as possible. You might decide to eat meat three times a week and make sure it's humanely raised and minimally processed, so that your conscience is clear on two counts. You might decide that if you're only going to have a glass of wine a day, then that wine is going to come from somewhere special and be the soul of ambrosia. Food would be elevated from the status of fuel to the status of art, and consuming it would be more ritualized. You'd make a point of sitting down to dine whenever you could, and anybody you hosted in your home would feel not just fed or even indulged, but privileged that you were sharing something intimate with them. Food would become your "thing," part of what made you interesting, and your kitchen would become a happy, if not sacred, place. Assuming you had the time and the taste for all this, life would become, quite simply, better.

Obviously, expressing yourself in a similar way through your sneakers, or your luggage, or your conditioning shampoo seems much less noble than doing it with beautiful food. I know this is a hard sell. Yet is buying a trunkful of whatever's on sale really any different than supersizing your Big Mac Extra Value Meal? If you ask me, the dividends of making your consumption more personal look pretty similar, whether you're talking about legumes or leggings. By being more careful, we are less wasteful. By paying attention to provenance, we encourage quality. By owning our choices we also own the consequences, which makes us more conscientious about our own well-being and the planet's. With all that altruism comes some real pleasure. When you hold everything you buy to the standards you set for yourself, everything you own is a delight and, frankly, makes you look good, too. Your stuff is a testament to what you're all about and your travels in life, rather than to your impulse control problem. When you're loading up the folding tables at your next garage sale, and you ask yourself, "What was I thinking?" the answer is probably that you weren't.

That's just the beginning of the good we can accomplish by thinking of consuming as curation rather than as acquisition. The best part, the biggest effect, will be in how those corporate cows will react when we do. By buying to express ourselves, we're feeding our values right back into our system of commerce. One citizen and one vote at a time, what motivates our buying eventually motivates the corporations that sell us things. Here's how.

The idea that a corporation will do whatever works actually extends far beyond our reaction to a product's design, its price, where it's sold and how it's promoted. In fact, many marketers see very little potential in setting a brand apart on the basis of those factors any more. As we've seen, not only is it hard to make something "best," it's hard to find a group of consumers of any commercially useful size who would agree on any definition of the word. That leaves marketers with two options: either aim to be a universally appealing commodity, and get very good at making things cheaper than anybody else, or find a way to identify with consumers that's more personal. Most experts on the subject agree that the latter is the only way to run a sustainably profitable business, and the only way to brand it. The battleground isn't value any more, it's values. Yours. Brands today are very interested in figuring out how they can connect not to your need to mow your lawn, but to your motive for doing it. How does a tidy lawn fit into your self-image? How do you relate philosophically to the tools you choose for chores like that? Your answers might account for 0.1 per cent of the reason behind your choice of garden tractor, but to a marketer that 0.1 per cent is all it takes to tip the teeter totter their way.

What's interesting about this, and what marketers perhaps didn't anticipate, is that trying to connect to us on that level raised our expectations of them. If all that matters is the product, it's fairly easy for a marketer to remake itself every year simply by bringing out "new and improved" products. Many packaged goods brands have stayed squarely with that strategy. Procter & Gamble, for example, with its relentless, long-standing focus on product development, built an empire on it. However, if a brand is going to claim that its values are aligned with ours when it comes to feeding the dog or putting tires on our car or going for our morning jog, it can't afford to change its stripes too often or capriciously. If it did, we would judge it the way we'd judge each other for doing the same thing: we would dismiss it as trivial and flaky, exactly the risk BMW ran when they put fashion ahead of their brand's heritage. So this approach to branding comes with some burdens for the marketer. They have to watch and listen carefully to know who their customers are and what they value, and they have to be consistent in the way they conduct themselves in order to prove their authenticity. When brands are based on values, their power comes from us, and that means they really have to be who they say they are. Over time, in other words, we make them in our own images, while they are forced to become, frankly, less slippery.

And do brands actually listen? Does values-driven branding work? The fact that it's a long-standing tradition suggests that it does. Here and there, throughout the age of advertising, famous brands have often become that way by selling what they stood for rather than what they made. The iconic Volkswagen ads of the early 1960s cast the die, giving that brand an ethos that, at the time, was far more attractive than the strange little car they were selling. (Putting the word "Lemon" above a picture of your product, as they once notoriously did, hardly flattered the car, but if you liked the ad's attitude, you were probably going to like the Beetle.) Inside the ad business, the proof most often cited is the launch of the Apple Macintosh in 1984, with a now-legendary television commercial that, rather than selling anything, was a manifesto declaring, in effect, that computers should serve humanity, not the other way around. Long before their product was a mass-market contender, Apple's brand empire – and its loyal, lucrative following – was built on an ideal.

Meanwhile, at the mall, triggered by the recession of the early 1990s, we in the marketing world started to observe that people were decoupling their brand choices from their socio-economic standing. In fact, they were becoming downright unpredictable, spending lavishly on some things and stingily on others to the point where it was no longer easy to guess a consumer's status by what they bought. After watching consumers fill their fridges with gourmet mustard and then buy store-brand ketchup on special, we at first assumed this was just an economic coping strategy and gave it a name: "scrimp and splurge." As the decade unfolded, though, people like McCracken and Rushkoff began suggesting that something much bigger and more fundamental than that was happening here. Prodded as much by the shifting zeitgeist as by necessity, people were deciding to spend their money more selectively, and that meant making choices that were personally rather than tribally motivated. And the habit has stuck.

The idea that there could be profit in connecting with consumers at this level is changing marketing radically, if slowly, and the impact of the change is being felt all the way to the

CEO's office. Why? Because a corporation's brand happens to be a significant component of its market value. A boardroom rule of thumb for a brand's contribution to enterprise value has long been 10 per cent, but the reality of today's brand-driven marketing environment is that it is often much, much more than that. CEOs, who in publicly traded companies are usually richly rewarded for increasing the value of their stock, pay attention to this kind of thing, and if they're paying attention so are their organizations. In the industrial past, a corporation could increase its value by being good at making things and by controlling the means of production. It could prosper with great management, and that 10 per cent was a bonus for having a good name. Soon, if not now, that same corporation's worth is going to depend on how many of us trust what it stands for. Our desire to express our own values partly through conspicuous consumption is forcing corporations to understand and respect those values, because their bottom line – and the boss's bonus – depends on it.

And if those corporations should lose their way, they need only consult a list of the world's most valuable brands for inspiration, like the one published annually by the consulting firm Interbrand. They'll be impressed by how many of the world's most admired and trusted brands are also worth the most money to the corporations that own them, and by how those brands are known as much or more for their ethos as for how their products work. Apple is a perennial winner in these contests. So is Toyota, with its dogged pursuit of flawless practicality; Google, with its mission to organize and make accessible all the information in the world; and personality brand darlings like Target and Southwest Airlines, with their missions to remake low cost into consumer empowerment. The wealth in these brands comes from having the most resonant characters, and the clearest sense not just of what they make but also of why we're supposed to believe they make it. When we consume as a form of self-expression, we have to share a brand's values before we'll spend money on it, which means we aren't just being more mindful consumers, we're actually helping shape the companies we buy from.

To me, in the end, this was the little epiphany of the 5brand experiment. Could any of us really define ourselves using just five brands? Obviously not. We'd be ridiculous and terribly shallow creatures if we could, though I'm also quite sure we could all speak the language and play the game just as well as the people in black did. No, what fascinated me was the revelation that the brandmakers are willing and able to curate their own inventions to describe themselves. They're confessing that these labels have become culture, and that their meaning has become social. It stands as proof, somehow, that consuming actually can be a personal act of creation, and that what ends up being created is not just a portrait of ourselves but of the kind of world we want to live in.

———

It doesn't take an anthropologist to see that New York City offers a glimpse of what consumerism might look like someday. To understand what I mean, though, you have to first get past the stereotypes about the city – that only very wealthy people live there, that it's aggressively status-driven, and that it's a temple to voracious consumption. Once you set aside all of this and walk the streets, even in the most plainly affluent neighbourhoods, a different picture starts to emerge.

You begin to realize that it's very hard to figure out any-body's social standing just by looking at their stuff. For one thing, ostentatious display is difficult to pull off. It's not a city of big homes and groomed lawns, not a place where you can guess at someone's disposable income by looking in their drive-way. So many souls live there in so little space that relatively few bother owning real estate or a car. Even if they do, odds are that their real estate is an anonymous box in the sky, and their car is buried underground in a concrete bunker. For another, life is just plain expensive. New Yorkers spend more of their income on housing than almost anybody in North America, so what people buy with the remainder of their money is surely more considered. For yet another, there is simply infinite vari-ety, of everything imaginable. There seems to be no cuisine, no article of clothing, no book or music, no appliance or piece of furniture that's more than a subway ride away. And, finally, people are more apt to be subversive about making a statement with their stuff. It's a place where off-duty movie stars are as likely to stroll around looking like bums as striving wannabes are to drip with branded ornament.

With less money to spend, less space to live in, and infinitely more choice, New Yorkers have developed a language for con-spicuous consumption that's richer and more subtle than you'll find in most places. So, if you want to figure somebody out, you have to get close. You have to talk to them. You have to assem-ble the clues they offer you. You can't write anyone off at a glance. Caught between the futility of trying to compete for bragging rights in a city where there's so much money, and the impossibil-ity of display in a city where the stage is so crowded, many New Yorkers seem to have decided somewhere along the way that being interesting is a better use of their energy than keeping score.

Which brings us back to those teenagers among the masto-dons. What they understood and the citizens of New York City seem to understand – and what millions of other consumers asking themselves hard questions in the wake of recession are beginning to realize – is that it's a big, complicated world out there, and that the only thing you can really call your own, the only thing you really have any control over, is your *self*. Status-driven consumption is an obsolete, not to mention simplistic and impractical, construct in contemporary life. We aren't born into the brand of jeans we wear and we aren't fated by our tax bracket to drink a certain brand of beer or drive a certain car. These are matters of choice. Choosing, even at the mall, is a creative act, and so it should be as deliberate as an artist's brushstroke.

Or, for that matter, anything you bought when you were sixteen.

CHAPTER SEVEN

AT THE MALL WITH BUDDHA, RUSKIN, AND MORRIS

Like everybody else, the marketing world would spend most of 2009 holding its breath. Although by then the recession was old news to economists, for the average person this was the year *It* happened. And unlike the previous couple of major economic downturns, this one seemed to be hitting people at the very heart of what made them feel safe and prosperous. In recessions of yore, you had a job or you didn't, and on that fact rested the security of your home. Now, it seemed that even the most securely employed person on the planet could still end up with a foreclosure sign nailed to the front door. This was new. It was hard to say with certainty how long it would last, or what things might look like when it was over. So, consumers, even the ones who still had jobs, choked off discretionary spending and borrowing to the extent they could. And marketers, while they waited along with the rest of us, assumed a defensive posture by advertising less, competed by discounting, and fired their ad agencies so that heads could be seen to have rolled. Every time networks filled unsold commercial time during *Law and Order* by running the same public service ads over and over again was a reminder that times were tough.

But you can't keep a good cow down for long. By fall, there seemed to be a light at the end of the tunnel, and the odds were improving that the light wasn't a train. Just as in one of those old cowboy movies where the good guy sticks his hat on the end of a rifle barrel and waves it around to see if the bad guys are out of ammunition, marketers began the journey back to normal by commissioning market research to find out exactly what normal was now going to look like.

In the research I was involved in, at least, the answer was pleasantly, surprisingly rational. Consumers weren't paralyzed by anxiety or even anger. Mostly, they were simply realistic and resigned. Nobody seriously thought that the last year or two had been an anomalous blip in our economic lives, or that life would – or should – ever go back to the way it was for most of the past decade. Life, consumers were certain, would never be the same again. Moreover, there was a strong sense among North American consumers that, though things would eventually get better, it was going to be up to them to make it happen. People knew they would need to lower their expectations. Yet, faced with that challenge, tempered optimism was what they were feeling most strongly. (Interestingly, this was especially true of those former '90s teenagers who, as it turns out, really did hang on to their provisional, self-reliant, individualistic approach to living, giving them the most confidence of any generational cohort that they would successfully adapt.) Everyone knew the game had changed. Governments and giant corporations had each had their failed turn at bat, and now it was the consumer's turn.

Nowhere was this sense of mission clearer and more focused for people than at the mall. In redefining normal, consumers weren't just committing themselves to a yoke of self-denial. They wanted to be different, to adapt not just by taking the pain but also by being principled. They were promising themselves they would make no purchase that was not, as one researcher put it, "considered," and that "carefree spending [would be] a thing of the past." Consumers were not just saying they would work harder to save money, avoid debt, and buy things at the lowest possible price. They were saying they were going to question themselves about the things they bought. They were going to test their urges against their own definition of need. Indeed, one survey raised eyebrows in the marketing world by revealing that almost half of Americans – in the middle of 2009's economic crap storm – believed that they had all the material possessions they needed in life, *up* from about one-third two years earlier when the economy was booming. They had a new priority: freedom.

Still, like a New Year's Resolution, the will to change can be helpless against the reality of old habits, temptation, and a short memory. There's a reason gyms are full in January and ghost towns by March. History tells us that we are more than capable of living life in a purposeful way, but it also tells us that we can get soft pretty fast in the absence of an immediate threat. The Depression produced the Greatest Generation; "irrational exuberance" produced Bear Stearns.

So how do we avoid backsliding when things get better? You can be sure that those marketers, reading the tea leaves for signs of recovery, are hoping against hope that the future will be like the past, only bigger. They won't be any help. How can we take this moment of clarity to the mall with us, now and always, and drag the cows into a new normal that is economically and environmentally, in every sense, sustainable? The answer is not to go alone. By this I do not mean that you should haul along whatever friend, relative, or life partner will most effectively throw a wet blanket on your consumeristic spasms of lust. No, I'm talking about companions of a more metaphysical sort, companions I have named Buddha, Ruskin, and Morris. Like Dickens's Christmas ghosts, their form is merely a convenient metaphor for the messages of possibility they bear.

Allow me to introduce you.

———

Stephanie Nolen is a Canadian journalist who has seen some of the harshest faces of humanity. She has been a foreign correspondent in some of the world's ugliest war zones and is a tireless crusader on behalf of those who live in its most benighted corners. Like every great reporter I've ever met, she has a healthy suspicion of consumerism, marketing, and the cynical things corporations do in the name of profit. Like fewer of them, she has managed to preserve a genuine humanity, a sense of humour, and a willingness to take the world as it is even while she's trying to change it. She wears no hair shirt (but takes girlish delight in her tailor-made French flak jacket with the suede epaulets), does not sit in smug judgment of the bourgeoisie, and only strengthens her fierce point of view by being endlessly curious and pragmatic.

So when, via Twitter, she shared the news that she would receive an honorary doctorate from the University of King's College, her undergraduate alma mater, and address the graduating class in the spring of 2009, I wondered what she would say. In fact, so did she – the news came attached to a plea asking friends what we wished we'd known when we were graduates ourselves. Here was a person with immense moral authority, someone who had received an Amnesty International Award for

Human Rights Reporting for bravely shining a light on things the world didn't want to see, and she was going to face an auditorium full of young people about to inherit "this mess," as she would put it to them. The obvious approach might have been to challenge them to fix it. Alternatively, I wondered if maybe she would offer them some pearl of hope for the species, which would be all the more potent considering her platform. Hope makes great commencement speeches.

Instead, Stephanie Nolen talked about her iPod.

To the graduating class of 2009, she said this:

. . . even if you spend the rest of your life right here, you are responsible for much of what happens elsewhere in the world. For how those other people live. Regardless of what you choose to do with your new degree, your new skills, you will be responsible.

If you have an iPod like mine, or a cellphone, or a Wii, you are connected to the 14-year-olds I have met who are enslaved by rebel groups in the Congo and who dig for coltan, the mineral that is the essential ingredient in our gadgets.

If you have a Gap T-shirt like I do, then you are connected to the Bangladeshi women who stitched it for five bucks a day, and who cannot develop their textile sector into better-paying jobs because of our trade restrictions . . .

And if, like me, you enjoy the occasional Starbucks latte, you are connected to the women in Ethiopia who earn 70 cents a day sorting their coffee beans. Ah-hah, you think. I always order the fair trade blend. Well, great. The women in the fair trade factory earn 96 cents a day. I know – I spent an afternoon on a Starbucks factory line in Addis Ababa, Ethiopia, a couple of years ago.

So I can tell you that those women are glad to have their jobs.

I'm not sure that's good enough.

You are connected to these people. And you decide how much responsibility you will take for that.

Her intent, I realize, was simply to make those shiny new King's College grads realize that their responsibility for humanity is omnipresent and inescapable. But I think the same message could serve equally well as a broader one for a much larger audience: If you are a consumer, you are a citizen of the world. You and the people who made the things you buy are all in this together. That's our first companion, the one I'm going to call Buddha: connectedness.

The problem with the typical rhetoric of anti-consumerism is that it exhorts people to *dis*connect. It leaves the reasonable person with nowhere to go with their urge to change things. No meaningful action to take. No way to begin. The passion and polemical heat of the people who bring us evidence of consumerism's damage to the world are matched only by the ringing absence of an alternative to the status quo. We hear all that's wrong – and make no mistake, plenty of it *is* wrong – but the relentlessness of it, uninterrupted by any hint of a way out, makes us shut down.

With environmentalism, at least, there was the blue box. Recycling provided an easy first step that everybody could take, an on-ramp to the possibility of more change down the road. You could sort your cans and bottles, carry the box to the curb on garbage day, look up and down the street at boxes just like it, and feel like you were part of something good. The blue box might be followed by a box for papers, then a compost bin. And so on. Nobody would be perfect. Nobody would sell their three-bedroom backsplit and live in the woods foraging for nuts and berries, but progress would be made. What had begun as a change in everyone's weekly routine gradually became normal and expected. But if your goal is to reform consumerism, the first step has always seemed less obvious – or less practical – and the process much less attractive.

For proof, consider the case of Britain's Neil Boorman. On September 17, 2006, the style-obsessed young event promoter, professing himself to be clinically addicted to brands, burned all of his branded possessions in a public bonfire. The bonfire, which was well attended by the media, was meant to launch an experiment that he would then chronicle in a book. After "twenty years of brand shopping and eighteen months of therapy," Boorman was going to live absolutely brand-free for six months, an act that he equated to an alcoholic pouring his booze down the sink, and one that would provide a moral example to us all. In the days and weeks that followed, blogged in real time, the public was able to observe his difficult, thought-provoking, funny, and sometimes pathetic struggle to avoid anything with a name on it. Boorman wears army surplus clothing, drinks water from the taps in pub bathrooms, concocts his own gritty toothpaste, and, in the process, exiles himself.

You are at first impressed by the truth of how hard it is to escape the gravitational pull of branded life, especially for a trendy young Londoner. Then a couple of things begin to dawn on you. You realize that Boorman doesn't know, or always care, about the provenance of the unbranded products he uses or who is responsible for them – a no-name substitute for his beloved Helmut Lang jacket is one thing, but the anonymous, slippery toilet paper from a janitorial supply company is rather more unsettling. (His wife maintains her own cache of the branded kind, and Boorman "occasionally creep[s] into the bathroom to feel the stuff between my forefinger and thumb; so soft, so velvety.") The process puts him into a kind of isolation. Neil Boorman bought less stuff, which was good. But by taking the extreme step of avoiding brands, he became disconnected from our system of commerce, effectively giving up his ability to influence it. And that made the entire experiment, besides being next to impossible, pretty much futile.

In fact, the easy first step towards mindful consumerism not only doesn't demand we wear a hair shirt, it actually forbids it. The first step is actually even easier than recycling was: Connect. There is no golden wall separating us from the provenance of the products we buy. There are no elves making our DVD players and La-Z-Boys out of fairy dust in magical workshops. Our consumption begins not in stores, but in factories, fields, and mines. We are an integral – *the* integral – part of a system that produces this stuff. A system made of imagination as well as exploitation. A system made with hands and sweat and ambition and banditry and creativity and rank opportunism. As Stephanie Nolen said, we are responsible. As Neil Boorman proved, we can't escape it. Without a doubt, our influence in that system is going to be greater and more positive if we acknowledge that we're part of it. Without a doubt, we'll make better, more personal choices if we feel that way.

The important thing is simply to begin. The fact is that most of us are unlikely to start knitting our own MP3 players or to march about with placards decrying the provenance of Sesame Street Potty Elmo, much as both might be worthy pursuits. Most of us probably won't even put the time into researching such things or, anyway, not at first. But we can read a label.

We can turn things upside down and begin to discover their stories. Looking around me as I write this, for example, I learn to no surprise at all that my MacBook, my iPhone, and my LaCie external hard drive all came from China. My Hugo Boss wallet, a gift from my wife, turns out to be from Italy, despite the brand's Teutonic origins. To my delight, I discover that my coffee cup hails from the Pioneer Pottery company in Ohio, a day's drive from where I'm sitting. My Herman Miller Aeron Chair (okay, yes, I'm *that* guy) was made in a facility in Holland, Michigan. The factory turns out to be Leadership in Energy and Environmental Design (LEED)–certified, and was honoured by the United States Green Building Council. While I was poking around on their website, I ended up watching a short video by the designer of my chair, the charming and plain-spoken Bill Stumpf, who passed away in 2006. I liked him. I'm glad to know the story of my chair, even if I got more than I bargained for. And, frankly, I look a little askance at Apple's "designed in California" feint.

Everything we have comes from somewhere. Everything we own started out as an idea, was touched by human hands, travelled the oceans and highways of the planet, and took its tolls along the way. And the fact is that, like Stephanie Nolen's iPod, Gap tee-shirt, and Starbucks coffee, and like all the stuff on my desk today – and unlike Neil Boorman's toilet paper – a brand gives us a place to start discovering its story and who's responsible for it. Just thinking about that changes the way you look at your belongings. It connects you to them. Just thinking about your stuff that way is the first step to conscientious consumerism.

The next is deciding what we should expect from it.

———

"There is hardly anything in the world that someone cannot make a little worse and sell a little cheaper, and the people who consider price only are this man's lawful prey." So, once upon a time, said signs on the walls of Baskin Robbins ice cream stores all over North America (proving again that wisdom is where you find it, and can be served in either a dish or a waffle cone).

The words are widely attributed to Englishman John Ruskin, who was one of the big-deal social thinkers of the nineteenth century. His life's work covered what we would today consider an improbably enormous amount of intellectual real estate. He was an author, poet, and painter, as well as a vigorous critic of architecture and art and a provocateur for economic reform. But, like the friendly folks at Baskin Robbins, we're going to focus here on a single, conveniently narrow theme in Ruskin's opus: quality. Although his writings on the subject of industry and economy were essentially socialist, Ruskin didn't think anybody should get a free ride. He didn't believe that society was morally bound to distribute work equally to every tradesman. Rather, he thought work should go to the people who did it best. "The proper reward of the good workman," he wrote, "[is] to be chosen." I think you could replace the word "workman" with the word "brand," and you'd have a fair description of how this selfsame process works in an era of mass production and consumption, or ought to. So, his lefty politics aside, Ruskin is the name we're going to give to our second companion at the mall, a conscience for quality.

Although product quality may not be something you hear much about when corporations come under fire for being bad citizens or when consumers are criticized for their profligacy, it's actually ground zero in the war between marketers and consumers. I would even go so far as to say that if it's not the main battlefront in the planet's fight for survival, it is most certainly a strategically vital front. The making of things, not the using of them, is often where the most environmental damage is done. And the root of the problem is often our own low expectations of those things and the odd priorities we set for ourselves when we decide what to spend on them. In our quest to get more for our money, we take quality for granted. Yet the quality of most consumer products, no matter what we or J. D. Power may wishfully think, is not something determined by an objective standard or arbitration. Quality is a moving and relative target, driven upward sometimes by innovation and downward sometimes by our own reluctance to pay for it. Very often in the world of marketing, the standard for quality is simply a matter of what the consumer will tolerate.

That last point is important, because profit, boiled down to its essence, is the difference between what it costs a company to make something and what consumers seem willing to pay for it. This is, without a doubt, among branded marketing's least pretty truths, because it puts a great deal of the onus on us.

On the face of it, there's nothing wrong in this equation, the notion that there's a difference between cost and value. We all earn our livings on the back of that premise, if we're honest with ourselves. Profit is not a crime, and value can be added to a product extrinsically, whether it's by something tangible, like convenience and customer service, or by something intangible, like prestige. A marketer can make a product more attractive without making it objectively better, and we can be the judges of whether the effort is worth paying for. That's fair ball, and it's certainly possible for everyone to go home happy when both sides play their parts. But if we as consumers take our eyes off that ball altogether, the equation changes. Our complacency becomes a resource to be exploited.

And what a resource. Complacency about product quality is a bonanza for every corporate scoundrel who sells anything from tee-shirts to televisions. You see, if a marketer were to succeed in making flat-out junk appealing to us, not only could he increase that spread between the cost of making it and the value we perceive it to have, but he could also increase the frequency with which we'd have to replace the damn thing. If we were talking about toasters, for example, this might mean the difference between our having to buy a new one every five years versus every ten. Poor product quality in that hypothetical example effectively doubles the size of the market for toasters without adding a single customer, besides likely improving the bottom line in each transaction along the way, not to mention doubling the planetary cost of building twice as many of the cursed appliances. If consumers didn't have the weapon of free choice to point at marketers, or if we were just utterly complacent about the quality of the stuff we bought, marketing would probably devolve into a race to the bottom. If someone thought they could sell us new disposable toasters every week without consequences, they would be right there on the shelf alongside the bread that goes in them.

What regulates this behaviour is the conversational nature of marketplaces. We are not victims of this math; we're elements in it. Our silent acceptance of the status quo is as good as a ringing endorsement, as far as a corporation is concerned. The corporate cow is just doing what works. It has been continually testing the limits of our tolerance since the very dawn of mass production, and calibrating them is the key to its prosperity. The concept of planned obsolescence appears as a common theme in the history of business strategy from at least the 1920s. Kettering's "ongoing creation of dissatisfaction" is certainly a cousin to this logic, and the business strategy of his employer – General Motors – was certainly rooted in the assumption of routine, frequent product replacement. Cars, as a twentieth-century consumer phenomenon, were designed to become disappointing embarrassments at regular intervals, kind of like the width of a man's tie, and countless other products have been marketed to us using that strategy. Every marketer's secret fantasy, in fact, is to have his product category become fashionable, for therein lies the promise of an endlessly unsatisfied customer.

Still, the art of marketing is rarely so simple, or at least not for long. Branded marketing isn't like some carpetbagger who rides into town one morning, spends the day swindling everybody out of their seed money and then disappears into the night. Marketers have to keep going back to the same town, over and over. The more often they can get away with it, the better for them, certainly. But they also know that they can wear out their welcome, and there's no money in that. Each time they come back, they need us to be as happy, or at least as willing, to see them as we were the last time. The marketer doesn't singlemindedly set out to screw us; he's just constantly attending to how much better than acceptable his product absolutely needs to be in order for him to stay in business. That means that he can't afford to ignore us for a second. It's also why our tolerance is tantamount to endorsement.

Our own influence over this process can be absolutely transformational. We don't even need to leave General Motors' Detroit to see the proof.

When I was a kid, cars were redesigned every year. It was a big deal. Guys talked about new lineups over backyard fences each fall as though car companies were hockey teams.

Horsepower went up and up, along with size. It became common practice – expected, even – for a typical middle-class family to trade their behemoths in every couple of years. Warranties were brief. Cars were so disposable that not only could a teenager like me afford to drive a five-year-old car on a pump jockey's wage, but he could also rely on junkyards to find parts to keep it going. A five-year-old car was old, and would likely spend much of its time with its hood up. And, thanks to the convenient miracle of oxidation, the evidence of its short life wouldn't linger too long.

Today, that's unimaginable. A five-year-old car is not only perfectly acceptable in most social circles, it's often indistinguishable from a new one. Even a ten-year-old car, if it's well cared for, is unlikely to attract much opprobrium from automotive snobs. Most models are redesigned every few years, now, rather than every year. A large part of the market, in fact, could probably not reasonably be called fashion-driven any more, not by comparison to the bad old days. Meanwhile, warranties last for years instead of months, and rusty cars are becoming a bit of an oddity, despite the best efforts of road salt–loving municipal governments. For consumers, the car market has almost nothing in common with its counterpart of thirty years ago. Just about everything about it is better. So what changed? The short answer: our standards.

Up until well into the 1970s, we were willing accomplices in Detroit's ambition to market cars as if they were sneakers. Then along came an oil crisis, and along came Japan, and along came cars that were less garish and better made. People bought them, partly out of necessity and partly in protest. In short order, the biggest, most capital-intensive, nation-building industry in all of branded marketing was brought to its knees. As a student around the time all this was hitting the fan, I had a summer job on the line at Ford's Talbotville, Ontario, assembly plant. I clearly remember the line being shut down one steamy day in August and our shift being gathered in the cafeteria of the plant to hear someone from head office harangue us about the growing threat. "The Japanese have almost a quarter of the market now," he said ominously, "and they're winning on quality. We have to do better." Mr. Ruskin might argue that he was talking to the wrong workers, but he would most certainly have agreed with the message – a message that was being sent by consumers from showrooms across the land, where they were loudly voting with their money.

Even with the moderating effect of brands, the battle over quality is a long way from over. The making of consumer products has been exported overseas for years, now, all in the quest for lower production costs. Chinese factories, for example, are famous for their determination to keep their costs the lowest in the world, and quality is always at risk when any enterprise, anywhere, is so single-mindedly focused on costs. Some people even believe that compromising quality is systemic in China. In a 2007 piece for *Esquire* magazine, blogger and author Colby Buzzell, on a quest to understand the place, quoted resident foreigners as claiming that the Chinese considered inferior product quality a duty because it ensured the jobs of future generations of workers. Polemical hearsay though it may have been, even the possibility is chilling.

That's why Ruskin, our conscience for quality, should be our constant companion at the mall. The ghost of a dead socialist, in addition to being a pretty good ice cream salesman, is not a bad moral compass for behaviour in a free consumer market. He reminds us that demanding better instead of demanding more is *our* duty. If we buy stuff that works and lasts, we end up buying – and spending – less over the course of our lives. If we buy stuff that works and lasts, we end up consuming fewer resources and filling fewer dumps. And if we buy stuff that works and lasts, we tell the cows in no uncertain terms what it's going to take to get us to part with our money the next time we go shopping.

———

Somewhere out there on the Internet, there is a guy named Dave. (Another guy named Dave, not Dave my philosopher mechanic.) His blog, conveniently, is called just that – guynameddave.com – and his mission is to evangelize for the spiritual benefits of having less stuff. Unlike Neil Boorman, though, Dave Bruno doesn't seem to need anyone to blame for our obsession with possessions. He believes that "American-style consumerism is the main bad habit holding back average folk in the U.S. from a productive and meaningful life. (If you doubt me, first check the status of your savings account and then check the status of your garage.)" The centrepiece of his crusade is something he calls "The 100 Thing Challenge." To set an example for mindful consumption, he committed himself to one full year of possessing just one hundred things, no more. Although it seems like a Boormanesque stunt on the surface of it, there is actually a gentle pragmatism about Dave's mission that I think makes it very persuasive. Dave, you see, doesn't look at the dilemma of consumerism primarily as a civic responsibility or an anti-corporate jihad. He looks at it as one of personal development. He calls consuming a habit, he sees it as the enemy of self-actualization, and he thinks the answer is to own less and buy it carefully.

Needless to say, I took the challenge. Okay, not really. I didn't actually reduce the number of my possessions to one hundred, but I did ask myself which hundred I'd keep, were I forced to so choose. The exercise was illuminating, because it ended up being so simple: To be considered for my list, a possession had to be either something I couldn't function without (my computer, say), or something I was emotionally attached to (my guitar, say). If something didn't qualify on either count (for example, my pop riveting kit, which I used only once and should have just borrowed instead of buying in a spasm of impatience), it suddenly changed in my eyes. I started thinking of it as so much dead weight, and I felt a little stupid about the space it was taking up in my basement.

To make matters worse, this whole exercise brought blushingly to mind an aphorism that I've used for years to browbeat untidy people in my life (you know who you are): "Have nothing in your houses that you do not know to be useful or believe to be beautiful." It's attributed to William Morris, a contemporary of Ruskin's, a fellow instigator of Britain's Arts and Crafts movement, and a fellow socialist. I have always loved this quote because it is so positive. It doesn't exhort us to suffer in self-denial. It exhorts us to make our consumption count for something. What Morris (the socialist) and Dave (who is probably not a socialist) seem to agree upon is that things should matter or there is no virtue in having them. Since Dave is still among us, and since his is probably too modest a name to give to a metaphysical being ("At the mall with Buddha, Ruskin, and Dave" doesn't have the same ring to it), I'm going to call our third companion at the mall Morris. Morris is about making it count.

The idea of usefulness needs little explanation or defence here. I think we know what we need, and "useful" and "useless" are fairly easy to tell apart. Something that's both useless and ugly is kind of a crime against humanity, and should languish in flea markets until nature takes it back and gives it another chance to be something worthwhile. The more challenging question has to do with the things we *want*, and it's here that the idea of believing something to be beautiful becomes important. The essential key to being happier with less is to ensure that the things we do invite into our lives are more satisfying, and for that they need to be in some way a joy to behold as well as to use. They should be the kind of thing we keep for a long time, objects that gather stories and patina and eventually become irreplaceable. Good design is not a vanity or a privilege reserved for rich aesthetes. Good design – whether it's a lamp or a socket wrench – is a consumer's inalienable right. And I think insisting on good design is one of the best pieces of insurance we have against buying too much, buying too often, and shipping our mistakes off to landfill sites in green plastic bags.

Visiting a museum with a great industrial design collection persuasively drives the point home. One of my favourites is New York's Museum of Modern Art. Its collection includes such ordinary things as a bicycle helmet, a skateboard tool, countless chairs, cellphones and computers, a soup tureen, a hairbrush, and a champagne bottle opener – all items that you once could have walked into a store and purchased some time or other over the last century. Looking around, one can't help but notice the sculpture of what were once simply somebody's branded products. Or the way the light catches a particular vacuum cleaner, or garden trowel, or swim fin, now under glass, curated and illuminated like the treasures of some ancient king. The care and thought that went into their design is suddenly obvious when you look at them like this. Someone, hunched over a drafting table once upon a time, decided to try to make a common object both useful and beautiful. The lesson? It's not always that things used to be more beautiful in the olden days than they are now. It's just that nobody bothered to keep the ugly stuff.

In forcing himself to stick to one hundred things, mind you, Dave Bruno did not indulge in much obvious ornament. Most of the items on his list had a functional purpose and, even then, it clearly wasn't easy to negotiate what would make the cut. But that doesn't mean there is no beauty in Dave's consuming life. What's striking about his list, which you can see on his blog, is that even the most useful of the things he keeps are still shown genuine appreciation. Many of them have a story (he dedicates an entire blog post to his REI sleeping bag and how camping inoculates him from his own laziness). Many of them are described by their brand names, making them more evocative (apparently not a fan of J. Crew, he confesses that one flannel shirt is so comfortable and enduring that he feels a bit badly about criticizing them). The list in its entirety – stories, brands, and all – becomes a sort of impressionist mosaic of who Dave is (someone whose faith is central in his life, an enthusiastic family man, a guy who writes and lives on-line, an avid camper). Like Grant McCracken's urban teenagers, Dave seems to be saying that the fewer things he has, the more they have to matter, and the fewer things he has, the more they have to represent him as much as they have to serve him.

At the end of the day, what's beautiful and what's useful are personal questions and we're all going to answer them in our own way. But imagine how delightful our homes would be – imagine how delightful *everything* would be – if we never again bought a single thing without first asking if it deserved to be there.

In the marketing world, there's an expression you sometimes hear used when a brand manager has discovered an opportunity to make people switch to his product. It's called "a teachable moment." It describes a point in time where we're especially susceptible to having our minds changed about something. A laundry detergent brand manager might see one in your kid's first day at school, when you suddenly become self-conscious about how clean your child's clothes look, the same clothes that looked normal and acceptable to you yesterday. A financial advisor might see one when a tax regulation changes; a snow tire brand manager might see one after an unseasonably early snowfall; a politician might sense one in a sudden, deep economic recession. Anybody with something to sell lives for that moment when the context around her product changes and suddenly shines a brighter, sharper light on what she was pitching all along.

No doubt, many brand marketers think that such teachable moments are in abundance right now, with the world changing as much as it is. But it seems to me that the biggest teachable moment of all might turn out not to be the one we're in, but the one *they're* in. No marketer I know is certain about what the future holds. No government or financial institution can say with conviction they know what consumerism will look like in the years ahead of us, given that everything that affects it – from employment to bank lending to environmentalism to our own social values – is in flux. In a very real sense, the corporate world is going to be holding its breath for a long time, waiting for the answer that only we can give them. What's obvious is that we're probably going to buy less in the future than we did in the past. What's less obvious are the terms on which we're going to do that.

It's these terms that our ghosts – the ancient monk and the two mouldering socialists – propose. We have before us the greatest opportunity of modern times to teach branded marketers what matters: to push the reset button on the whole system. If we make a point of connecting with the provenance of the brands we choose, says Buddha, the marketer becomes more accountable. If we demand only things that work and last, says Ruskin, that's what they have to make in order to stay in the game. And if we insist that the things we invite into our homes deserve to be there, says Morris (or Dave), they'll compete to make them more satisfying rather just cheaper.

And for the first time, every trip to the mall might make the world a little bit better instead of a little bit worse.

CHAPTER EIGHT

THOSE CRAZY EUROPEANS

Diamond-encrusted sinks are over, pronounced the *Wall Street Journal.*

They weren't the first to hop aboard this particular dour bandwagon when they published a piece titled "Spendthrift to Penny Pincher: A Vision of the New Consumer" just before Christmas 2009. Social commentators, researchers flogging their latest polls, and media outlets trying to explain away their decimated advertising revenues had been agreeing for months that our Troubles might permanently change the way people both look at and practise consumerism. These pronouncements carried a sort of puritanical undertone, as if to say that (a) we had it coming and (b) it's not going to be good. We were now all going to be dismally careful with our money, and the necessity of this was our punishment for years of credit-lubricated frolicking at the mall.

Although there were hopeful whispers of recovery by the time the *Wall Street Journal* article appeared, it was difficult to argue with their prognosis. Not only was our consuming life going to be different, we were going to have to change the way we thought about it. A scant year earlier, some of us had wondered secretly if the global financial meltdown was going to sweep us back to the Dark Ages, wherein we would wander the earth in furs and scratchy wool robes, foraging for berries and nuts. It had been, we suspected, a close call. But close, as they say, only counts in horseshoes. Our world didn't end and, if it had, it still wouldn't have been the worst self-inflicted wound our species ever endured. Still, all that anxiety raised an interesting question: What does consumerism look like *après le déluge*? When a society and its economy go through a massive reset, when our ceaseless march toward more is interrupted, what happens?

We don't have to go back further than what for some is living memory to see an example of a highly developed society suddenly and violently thrown backward by calamity. That, maybe too modestly, describes Europe in the middle of the last century. At every imaginable level, European society was laid to waste by the Second World War. With so much wealth and property destroyed, and so much economic infrastructure disrupted for so long, consumerism should have regressed to the protozoan stage. Yet soon after, and for much of the fifty years that followed, European markets produced consumer goods that were models of beauty, functionality, and durability. From cars to corkscrews, European products were often examples for the rest of the industrialized world. This renaissance was wrought not by a comfortable, safe society with disposable income but by people who had to content themselves with less and who were thus determined to demand better. And, somehow, in the end, having to start over also produced respectably robust industrial economies, with Germany, for example, becoming both the world's biggest exporter and third-largest economy, remaining so until it was overtaken by China in 2009.

Starting almost from square one, and in just a few decades, those crazy Europeans managed an industrial renaissance and created some very admirable stuff in the process. They became an economic powerhouse and, all the while, still managed to individually consume less than their North American peers. Some of us may not admire their big governments or their often left-tilting politics, and none of us wants their higher taxes or their six-dollar-a-gallon gasoline, but they obviously do know a few things we don't about how to make consumerism count for something. Here's what we *do* know: The average Western European today, while a little less economically productive (because he works less and vacations more), has less personal debt, saves more of what he earns, and produces a smaller carbon footprint than his North American counterpart, and feels more empowered in his relationships to corporations. Most importantly for our purposes, he's significantly more satisfied with his lifestyle. Sure, there may be differences we can't or don't want to emulate about life in the Eurozone, but that isn't one of them. A culture of people that is both more discriminating as consumers and happier in life, while remaining relatively prosperous and environmentally conscientious, sounds admirably like a consumer republic to me.

It turns out that there are some basic, human-level truths about the way Europeans consume – truths that are more about perspective than about ethnicity – that help explain this state of affairs.

————

To learn anything from the European approach to consumerism, we first have to let go of the notion that it's somehow a quaint imitation of North America's. People often make a sort of Ameri-centric assumption that the world's consumers all learned how to do it from us as a consequence of globalization. Whether you're in Amsterdam, Tokyo, Sydney, or Mumbai, it's very likely that the newest and shiniest things you come across today will also be the most familiar and will very likely be branded. It appears as though the nations of the world are relatively new to our ways, when it's really just the imperial spread of global brands – mostly North American in origin – that's new. In much of the developed world, however, consumerism had a long, inter-esting history before Starbucks arrived, and this is most point-edly true in Western Europe. The Europeans, in fact, all but invented consumerism. North Americans, as cultural historians will tell you, got their first lessons from them.

Roughly defined as the practice of buying things you don't need and doing so for the specific purpose of being seen to have them, consumerism, as we would recognize it, has European roots dating to the late seventeenth century. It's thought that one of the first products produced in quantity for this kind of com-merce was sugar. Once it entered the home of a socially ambi-tious European, this delectable commodity in turn created demand for lovely tea and coffee accessories in which it could be shown off to guests. The parlour, where this display took place, would then need to be furnished with exotic carpets and other such fruits of colonialism; a fashionable wardrobe for entertaining would then become a concern; and so on, ad infini-tum. In other words, merchant-class European life in those days was a lot like middle-class life anywhere today. Right down to the resulting household debt.

The rise of a merchant class helped bring about this seminal consumerism. The export and import of goods and materials made it possible for people who were not hereditary aristocrats to accumulate some wealth, and much of Europe was operating economically above subsistence levels – a new phenomenon. A new stratum of society emerged as a result – the economic force that made consumerism *possible*; it was two cultural forces that actually *made* it happen. One was a desire to dismantle the strict class structure of the time. Put simply, by appearing to be richer than you actually were, you subverted the traditional caste system that had kept European society at a social standstill since the last Ice Age. Naturally, these consumers were aspiring to status, but there was more to it than that. Just as a hip-hop star driving a Range Rover and wearing Burberry deliberately undermines the exclusionary aristocratic status of those brands even while he enjoys their luxury, so the eighteenth-century European merchant used sugar, tea, coffee, and stylish clothes to undermine the rigid and stultifying social structure into which he'd been born.

The second force to promote the rise of consumerism there and then was a little thing called the Enlightenment, a philosophical transformation in the Western world occurring at about the same time, in which human reason and scientific inquiry began to challenge the notions of birthright and faith as the bases of social order. Religion had to make room for the secular and, as a result, conspicuous piety made way for conspicuous consumption. It would have been tough to argue that your swanky new tea service was in any way an expression of your faith, and altogether more satisfying and less socially risky to show it off when it could just speak for itself.

And it's here, embedded in this bit of history, that perhaps the central difference between European consumerism and North American consumerism presents itself, a difference that

I think endures as a cultural echo right up to the present day. Europe's embrace of consumerism, while certainly not without controversy along the way, took place in a larger, sweeping context of class revolution and secularization. It was, by comparison, unambiguous, and emblematic of social changes that were more fundamental. In North America, it was a more ambivalent thing, and this was especially true in what is now the United States. Among that country's most celebrated cultural inheritances is the Puritan one, and so tied is it to the theme of consumption that it supplies American Thanksgiving with most of its iconography. The Puritans came to the New World to escape secularization, and they were advocates of a more ascetic and faith-based life, an ideal that persists in the American psyche. Complicating things further, consumer goods – when they began to appear in America – were largely imported from its colonial ruler, and so the act of buying them inevitably became bound up in pre-Revolutionary politics. History records a speech, for example, made by an anonymous "Carolinian" to the Continental Congress in which he argues that "the man who would not refuse himself a fine coat to save his Country deserves to be hanged." It's no wonder that Americans have such mixed feelings about consumerism, and it would be surprising if Canadians, as their closest neighbours and avid consumers of their popular culture, didn't harbour the same doubts.

Simply put, Europeans have probably been more comfortable with consumerism not only because they've had longer to get used to it but because the unconscious cultural memory of it is largely a populist one. Here in North America, we have an unconscious cultural memory of consumerism as a form of economic slavery, a sign of moral weakness or even, for Americans, a crime against the Revolution. Opposition to it has been less intellectual and more evangelical. It's been, for us, a guilty pleasure from the start. We come by this ambivalence honestly, and it paints consuming as a naughty pleasure. Whereas those crazy Europeans have been relatively rational about the whole thing ever since their ancestors were showing off their sugar.

That's the first truth. As with so many other pleasures in life, Europeans in the main seem simply to have had fewer hang-ups about consumerism. It's just not tangled up in big culturally defining moral themes the way it is in the United States, where, even as the Declaration of Independence was proposing everyone's right to pursue happiness, the purchase of a new coat might have been a hanging offence. It's almost as though the more detached from moral themes consumerism is, the more moderately it's practised and the less ideologically divisive it is as a social issue. A social consensus that takes guilt out of the equation – as Europeans seem to have reached for, say, daily wine consumption and nude beaches – makes people less inclined to be judgmental, which, in turn, makes people feel less like they have something to prove.

Free of its connections to patriotism, politics, and morality, consumerism suddenly becomes less preoccupying, and our relationship to our stuff assumes more rational proportions. With less emotional static around our buying decisions, we feel less need to make statements with them, and somehow less temptation to be excessive. Eventually, as I suppose is the case with dropping your swim trunks on the French Riviera, you just don't think about it any more.

———

Certainly the citizens of Europe seem somehow more at ease with the art of living than we are. Film and television are consistent in their gauzy, romantic portrayal of the Old World as a place where people remember what matters. Even if it's only half true, there must be, I assumed, a basic and shared difference in values at work here. How else to explain the wistful clichés, the number of people who nurse *A Year in Provence* and *Under the Tuscan Sun* fantasies, or even just all the cool stuff Europeans have? And so I began digging to see if I could find the secret that accounted for this more evolved cultural state. And apart from the big differences I cited at the start of this chapter, and apart from the fact that private consumption really is a smaller percentage of Europe's gross domestic product than it is of North America's, the reasons behind Europe's apparently enlightened way of life remained stubbornly cloaked in mystery and contradictory evidence. Nothing came shining through that defined what made Europeans essentially alike yet different from North Americans, and at the same time explained their behaviour as consumers. Nothing.

As a matter of fact, Europeans seem to have next to nothing in common with *each other*, never mind with the rest of the world. In the face of the world's current economic travails, for example, Europeans don't even seem to agree on how to prioritize their household spending. In one study, people in the U.K. said they would be quick to cut back what they spend on personal health care if times got tougher, something the same study showed Germans wouldn't dream of doing. The Italians would only abandon spending on furniture and consumer electronics under great duress but would cut back on personal care items more readily, while the Brits would be quick to cut back on electronics and much slower to do so on furniture, and would be far more reluctant to cut back on personal care items than either the French or the Italians. So much for agreeing on "what matters." Values-wise, the more deeply you look into it, Europe doesn't seem to offer an example for us at all. If data could speak, it would be saying, "These people are too busy marching to the beats of their own regional drums to teach us anything."

Which, I finally realized, is the lesson.

As a social phenomenon, it's always seemed to me that consumerism occurs along two dimensions: a vertical one, in which consumption is a scoreboard for achievement or status, and a horizontal one, in which it's a medium for personal expression (as discussed in Chapter 6). Although this would be difficult and contentious to prove empirically, there seems to be a powerful inverse correlation between how much diversity exists in a society and how voraciously it consumes. In other words, the more we obsess about conforming, the more we seem to spend, whereas, for some reason, when we concern ourselves instead with what makes us unique (something Europe's constituent national cultures appear to keep a constant eye on), this urge seems to be suppressed a little.

This hypothesis seems plausible when we contrast North America to Europe, though it's fair to say that the more intrusive presence of government there and the higher taxes most Europeans pay explains some of their behaviour. At a glance, it would be easy to attribute their approach to consumption to their simply having less disposable income. The hypothesis becomes more interesting, though, when you look within North America. For example, Canada as a nation is committed to the idea of diversity almost by definition. It's pervasive in every government policy, from immigration to arts funding; it's one of the few sure things Canadians can cite when they try to define themselves; and it's plainly evident in the polyglot of its cities. If the country lacks something in terms of a defining idea, it makes a virtue of the resulting cultural incoherence. Individualism, the true cultural force underpinning diversity in Canada, is so sacred to the Canadian social contract that even expressions of patriotism can be a little uncomfortable outside certain prescribed contexts. Canadians are a pretty "me, then us" bunch, unless the chips are down. And guess what? Canada, like many European countries, has historically always had a significantly higher personal savings rate than the United States, despite having a more comprehensive social safety net. For that to be the case, consumer culture is surely less of a force north of the forty-ninth parallel than it is south of that border.

The U.S., meanwhile, though becoming more diverse all the time, remains fundamentally a highly successful revolutionary state. There are certain specific ideologies attached to being American that are consensual and conditional to good citizenship and that supersede the individual, and there are mechanisms – mass media, for example – that reinforce a general agreement on what it means to be an American. This is so pervasively true that marketers regularly reach for the word "America's" to attach to their brand of above-ground swimming pool or soluble fibre drink or microwave popcorn, certain in the knowledge that the collectivity embodied in that word will magnetically draw consumers together in reverent celebration. America is an "us, then me" place, even at the mall.

The United States and Canada are more essentially alike than either is to any other country on earth, right down to the way we're taxed. I doubt that there is a pair of national cultures that have more in common than these ones do – except for the social consensus around diversity and individuality. And it's hard to ignore the fact that the one that is united around a common vision of happiness seems to spend a little more at the mall, while the one that doesn't agree on much apart from hockey and doughnuts – the one that's somehow a little more European – has historically, at least, managed to put more money in the bank every month.

Okay, not very scientific. Yet it's interesting how often the connection between constrained consumerism and consuming for self-expression seems to present itself, from financially strapped Gen-X teenagers, to rent-poor New Yorkers, to one-hundred-things Dave. Somehow, just as having less seems to make us more individualistic in our choices, the reverse can also be true. The less group-driven we are in the way we consume, the less we seem to need. It seems reasonable to suppose that less really is more in this context. If consumption is a way of keeping score, then there's no such thing as too much – but if consumption is a way of distinguishing yourself rather than of conforming, "too much" means something else altogether. It means you're a glutton. That you're not discriminating. That you're trying to fill a spiritual hole with material things, exactly as Paul Nystrom fretted we might do.

One even wonders if that spiritual hole wasn't actually dug by the quest for conformity in the first place. The phrase "keeping up with the Joneses" can be traced back to a satirical comic strip of the same name, which appeared at about the same time as people such as Nystrom were worrying about the psychic cost of conspicuous consumption. Comparison in the context of conformity can be an ugly pathology. It makes us competitive. It makes us insecure. It makes us diminish what we have in the privacy of our own minds, and what others have in our public rhetoric. And it makes us sitting ducks for marketers. It can even confuse our moral compasses and our common sense. Worst of all, like the Joneses in that comic strip, who are never actually seen, the people we're comparing ourselves to are probably mirages anyway. There's no way our neighbours are as smug as they look with that fifty-four-inch plasma screen television, just as there's no way they're really using every one of those thousands of square feet they live in. In fact, by the end of the first decade of this century, you had to wonder if all this comparative consumption, powered as it was by money people didn't actually have, had gone meta on us. It seemed to have been driving us to the mall in throngs, not so that we could be seen to do better than our neighbours, but so that our *image* of ourselves could be seen to do better than what we assumed was our neighbours' image of *them*selves.

To one European culture, in particular, that game would be incomprehensible. In Jean-Benoît Nadeau and Julie Barlow's book *Sixty Million Frenchmen Can't Be Wrong*, there's an amusing passage about the ubiquity of shutters on the windows of French homes, and the way those homes, architecturally, often "turn their backs on the street." The roots of this apparently had to do with avoiding the attention of the taxman. In pre-revolutionary France, prosperous citizens carried the tax burden for the nobility, and their assessments were based on "apparent wealth." Agents of the state would, quite simply, look through your windows to see how much nice stuff you had, then make certain that you were taxed accordingly. This, you can imagine, would have discouraged the purchase of whatever was the pre-revolutionary equivalent of fifty-four-inch plasma screen televisions. Not surprisingly, it resulted in money matters remaining emphatically in, as the authors put it, "the private sphere."

Money is such a private matter in France that it's impossible to guess what someone earns by their occupation or their lifestyle. In any case, it would be as vulgar a subject of public discourse as sex can be in North America. The French, being human, certainly must compare themselves to one another on plenty of dimensions, but none of them is conspicuous wealth.

In the previous chapter, I suggested that by asking yourself whether something you're about to buy deserves to be in your home you will tend to modulate your spending and demand more of the brands you choose. Now, in addition to asking you to judge the beauty or quality of a product, I'm asking you to consider whether that product speaks for your *self*, rather than merely your *ambition*, and to settle for nothing less. Nothing will make you a more discriminating consumer than that question, egocentric as it may seem. As a citizen in a community, it's right and proper to share certain values with your fellow citizens and to be willing to subordinate yourself to those values now and then, for the collective good. But as a citizen of the consumer republic, the opposite is true. The collective good is very often best served by acting according to the values that are yours alone. On some level, to be that kind of good citizen, you have to decide that what other people think of your economic achievements just doesn't matter. You have to decide that the only scale that matters is the one that gauges your distinctiveness, that money and its trappings are a private matter, and that your glorious uniqueness is the only thing the world needs to see.

After all, five hundred million Europeans can't be wrong.

———

From among the pop culture legacies left us by *The Sopranos*, I think the greatest by far is its deadpan satire on American middle-class life. For all of its putative intentions as a post-modern crime drama, it's hard to ignore the arch portrait of its main character, Tony, as a striving middle-class guy, working his way up a corporate ladder and stuck on a financial treadmill imposed on him in equal parts by a parasitic family, the need to look successful in order to succeed, and a pathological urge to ease his psychic pain with self-indulgence. Tony Soprano has to keep working in order to succeed, and he has to make himself feel successful in order to keep working. He is incidentally a murderous sociopath; mostly, he's every salary slave that ever mortgaged himself into too much house and leased himself into too much car, thinking that spending it forward would both motivate and satisfy him.

So it's no surprise that branded products abound in the series, even though the producers claim never to have sold product placement opportunities to marketers. The social meaning of all that stuff had to be unmistakable, and uncomfortably familiar to us, for the satire to work. Brands were almost indispensable in that regard. Like stickers on a well-travelled suitcase, brands were used in the series as labels to help mark poor, hapless Tony's journey to spiritual oblivion. It was fair game. Since the very dawn of advertising, there is no tool of persuasion that Madison Avenue has reached for more frequently than the idea of branded goods as rewards for hard work. Everything from beer and spirits to cars and cigars has been sold to us on the premise that we have earned them. The connection between work, reward, and branded consumerism, it might even be argued, was the single biggest engine of the North American economy in the post-war period. A shiny new Buick didn't seem like too much to ask for saving the world, and before you knew it, buying ourselves something pretty whenever we thought we deserved it became a self-perpetuating habit.

A habit that Europeans, it turns out, might not completely share.

How Europeans view work and how we in North America do is one of the most striking differences between these two regions of the world. Americans, for example, work 15 per cent more hours in a year than people in Germany, France, or Italy, yet Europeans actually view work as being more important than Americans do (and when they're actually working, Europeans are more productive). One academic who studies happiness at the Institute for Quantitative Social Science at Harvard University extends the conundrum even further, demonstrating in one analysis that more work can actually make Americans happier, whereas it makes Europeans decidedly less so. The temptation, says the study, is to view this as a product of Americans' Protestant work ethic, for example, and as a function of the differences between the two regions' social contracts (things like taxation, the social safety net, and conventions around vacation time) and social mobility, which is more prevalent in America than in Europe (or almost anywhere else, it seems). Instead, the truth seems to be simpler than that: Americans, the study concludes, are happier to work longer hours because in the United States – and presumably in Canada – working hard is associated with success in life. That's a potent motivator in a society where success is meant to be observable or is maybe even conditional upon it. Let's imagine for a minute that this phenomenon, over time, becomes a social convention, and you can see Tony's problem. If you're working hard, you must be succeeding and therefore happy. If you're succeeding, you must be working hard, and therefore happy. And if that axiomatic equation for some reason stops working, it's no surprise that he, or you, or I, might head off to the mall to restart the cycle.

Those crazy Europeans, by contrast, seem to have a different definition of success in life, or a different need for that success to be observable, or some combination of the two. You only need to consider the all-important home to see what I mean. The average European occupies only about half as much living space as the average American does yet is markedly more satisfied with where he or she lives than the average American is, including, apparently, the Tony Sopranos in their 10,000-square-foot McMansions, swimming pools and all.

Pondering this bit of evidence, I was reminded of a Canadian friend of mine who several years ago was posted to a leadership position with a big corporation in the United States. The first time I visited him, he gave me a guided tour of his new home. I was gobsmacked. His house was enormous – you could fairly use the word "wings" to describe its outermost sections. Parked at the end of the long, winding, paved driveway were a gleaming SUV for the nanny to take the kids to school and a luxury sedan of the sort that makes you change lanes when you see it in your rear-view mirror. As long as I'd known my prosperous and upwardly mobile friend, he had never been into displays of affluence. So I called him on it. He said, with a resigned shrug, "It's just how it is here. I have a lot of people reporting to me, and I need them to perform. For that, I need them to see what success looks like."

That's how you know that we might be linking the way we consume to the way we make our livings just a little too closely. When envy becomes a leadership technique, it's time to ask ourselves whether maybe we're working for the wrong reason.

That brings us to another truth about conscientious consumption inspired by our friends across the pond: you have to have a healthy attitude about work, and be willing to separate what you do from who you are. Legions of New Age philosophers have told us for years that if we do something we love for a living, the money we need will come to us, and the rest of our rewards will be more spiritual and intrinsic. Being happy in our work, they suggest, means we'll need less in the way of material things. I'm sure there must be something to it. But what if we go further than that? What if we challenge ourselves to pick away at the connection between work and lifestyle until it's all but gone? It's hard to see how that could be anything but good. We'd almost certainly spend in more reasonable proportion to our means and compare ourselves to one another a little less ruthlessly. The European example seems to hint at the possibility that we could be happier. And maybe best of all, we'd deprive marketers of one of their most cherished tools for making us do silly things at the mall.

Not to mention the fortunes we'd save on therapy.

———

There was a time when not everybody bothered to have a cellular phone, but that didn't stop cellphone companies from dreaming of the day they would. So one year I found myself working for one of these companies, trying to figure out what was holding everybody back. In those days, money was the easy answer. Handsets were expensive and so was airtime. It was easy to see, though, that this was an excuse as much as a reason. There was obviously something deeper, an issue with social meaning. The cellular phone was firmly trapped in its characterization as a tool for business. In focus groups, people would say things like, "I can see this being useful if I were a real estate salesperson or a stockbroker, but it's not for me." So it went, in focus group after focus group. The cellular carrier tried desperately to find ways to make people see the product as "useful," and the consumer vigorously resisted the stereotype attached to it. Until, that is, we got to Quebec. In Quebec, North America's very own liberally buttered slice of old Europe, consumers were just as resistant to cellphones, but they were much more direct about why. The defining moment, for me, sitting there behind the one-way glass, happened in Montreal. The moderator of the group asked everyone at the table how cellular phones could be useful to them. There was a short pause, and then one person snorted, "They're very useful for recognizing jerks in restaurants."

That smart-ass remark was a turning point for cellular telephone marketing in North America and, significantly, it was all about point of view rather than about what the product could do. In English Canada, people were worried about their image. The idea of having a phone in your pocket or in your car was very attractive, but people didn't want to look too big for their britches. French Canadians saw the cellphone as a tool for work just like everybody else did, but its social meaning was to identify people who didn't know how to *stop* working. Which, in that culture, was nothing to be proud of. The key to selling cellphones in Quebec would turn out to be the key to selling them everywhere: Don't argue with consumers about how this product can make them more efficient in taking care of the business of their lives. Instead, reframe it as a social tool, a way to connect with the people they care about, without barriers. It seems so obvious now, twenty years on, but marketing is like that sometimes. The cow occasionally needs to be reminded that it's not all about the milk.

Across the pond, Europeans were arriving at the same conclusion about cellular phones, and far more rapidly, thanks to the cost of conventional telephony there. For most of the past two decades, in fact, they fetishized the little gadgets, spearheading the movement to design the product to look more like a toy or jewellery and less like a military field radio. European consumers resisted any design that made the phone seem like "gear," preferring internal antennas and handsets that looked more like candy bars than something out of *Star Trek*. Customs and rituals quickly developed around such questions as whether it was appropriate to put your "mobile" on the table at a restaurant (this varies, predictably, by country). In no time at all, the cellular phone became a more personal object than even a wallet or purse, something we've only recently begun to see in North America. A lot of marketers at the time glibly put this down to the fearless early-adopter tendencies of those crazy Europeans, what with their swoopy cars and daring fashion. But the truth, it seems to me, was not that they had embraced and adapted themselves to a new technology at all. Quite the reverse. Recognizing that these little phones could enrich the all-important social life that made working worthwhile, they found a place for them. Europeans didn't change who they were in order to accept this new technology; they used who they were as the criterion for accepting it. The culture drove the marketplace, not the other way around.

This, I think, is the real inspiration Europe has to offer the consumer republic. In the end, one of the most interesting things about the invention of post-war Europe was that in starting over, Europeans returned to cultural basics. Briefly and violently shed of the hubris and distractions of the modern age, it looks from here as if Europe simply returned to the essence of itself. Notions older than the twentieth century – the idea that what makes you different is more important than what you have (which is nobody's business anyway) and the idea that we work to live rather than live to work – seem to have asserted themselves, ensuring a unique stamp on what might otherwise have been a carbon copy of North American consumerism.

There's something to be said for that, for starting over. Long before anybody even thought of a diamond-encrusted sink, we, too, nurtured some pretty admirable cultural ideals about thrift and responsibility and humility, about being content with who you are, and about the risks of getting too big for your britches. Now might be a good time to stand up and shout those out. Now, while the media and marketing complex that enabled our current travails is trying to figure out what the future looks like. Now, while the financial institutions that fuelled it are still in a cautious mood. Now, while the world's biggest manufacturing economies are wondering when and how we're coming back to the mall.

They probably already know that we're as ready as they are to rebuild. What they need to hear is that, this time, we're going to do it old school.

PART THREE

PITCHFORKS AND TORCHES

WHY THE REVOLUTION WILL NOT BE TELEVISED

Dave Carroll (not to be confused with Dave my philosopher mechanic, or one-hundred-things Dave) is the front man of a musical act called Sons of Maxwell, a hard-working folk and country duo based in Halifax, Nova Scotia, where Dave and his brother Don are also firefighters. Their style of music – rootsy and earnest with a Celtic edge – is the kind of thing you can hear a lot of in Nova Scotia, so you know that for Dave and Don to make a go of this, they must have put their hearts into it. And indeed they did. Well before United Airlines broke Dave's guitar, they had made a very good name for themselves. They toured all over North America and as far abroad as China, winning a loyal audience and some prestigious music awards in their very competitive home market. They were doing just fine.

But in March 2008, United Airlines did break Dave's guitar. En route from Halifax to Omaha, Nebraska, the band caught a connecting flight in Chicago and, as they sat on the plane waiting to depart, they actually witnessed their instruments being thrown around on the tarmac by baggage handlers. Dave's 710 Taylor guitar was badly damaged, and United was, by all accounts, not very nice about it in the aftermath. The story of the next year of futile and infuriating letters and phone calls is widely available for reading on-line, including on Dave Carroll's own website. What matters here are not the letters and phone calls that went nowhere, but what happened when Dave Carroll finally gave up.

As luck would have it, I watched the whole drama unfold on Twitter the day it happened. I caught somebody's re-tweet about it and out of curiosity found myself scanning United Airlines' Twitter feed. United's corporate twitterer had apparently been apprised of the YouTube video entitled "United Breaks Guitars," which Dave had posted the previous day, July 6, 2009. Gamely, and obviously trying to kill the story, United tweeted in reply, "This has struck a chord w/ us and we've contacted him directly to make it right." But it wasn't going to be that simple. Because Dave's video was about to go viral.

Within a couple of days, the view count for Dave's YouTube video was up in the seven figures. Within a couple of weeks, it would be north of four million, roughly double the audience size for a good episode of *Mad Men*. United would offer Dave money and ask very politely if they could use the video for training purposes. Then "United Breaks Guitars" would rise to number one on iTunes, and United's stock price would plunge by 10 per cent, reportedly costing shareholders $180 million. Dave, meanwhile, had long since paid to have his guitar fixed, and so declined United's cash offer when it finally came, directing it instead to a charity. He knew karma had already repaid him many times over. And he knew that United had probably suffered enough.

It was, let's be realistic, a fluky story. It's unlikely that most of us will ever get results on this kind of scale by making our disappointments with a brand public, on-line or anywhere else. However, the episode proved two very important things about the consumer republic. It proved that we have a voice and the means to make it heard, and that corporations eventually have to listen to it. And it proved that none of us is an island in the marketplace, as witnessed by the cascading consequences of Dave's broken guitar – everybody got in on the act, from the guitar maker, who added services and advice for other musicians who fly with their guitars, to social media experts, who trotted the terrifying case into boardrooms around the world, to the news media, who performed their democratic duty by telling the world how one Nova Scotia folk singer put a giant airline into a public relations headlock. The marketplace is an ecosystem, and every agent in it – you, me, a folkie from Halifax – has at least some power to affect the entire system.

That's what this next and final section is about: being heard.

CHAPTER NINE

GOOGLE'S CESSPOOL

When the World Wide Web came to town in the early 1990s, people in the marketing world reacted in one of two ways. On one side was the majority, who believed that this technology was little better than a toy and would likely never have any commercial value. Partly, they believed this because the Web couldn't do much. It was difficult to make sense of the economics when you needed to spend thousands on a computer, pay monthly for Internet access, and wait minutes to look at what amounted to a poorly printed brochure, which you couldn't even then fold up and put in your pocket. Partly, too, marketers believed this because the only precedent for it, on-line services like CompuServe and Prodigy and America Online, had never seemed to amount to very much more than an expensive distraction for socially handicapped nerds. Marketing people, who focus on results this month, this quarter, this year, are grounded in the here and now, and somewhat hard-headed about it. The Web's potential, depending as it did on future technological revolution to become practical, was a pretty abstract thing.

Then there was the minority, a group of geeks and seers who somehow saw beyond the horizon. To their eternal credit, they were convinced that computers would get cheaper, that bandwidth would get cheaper and more bountiful, that connection speeds would increase, and, most impressively of all, that the Web would be a great leveller between corporations and the people they're supposed to serve. What the Web would do, they said, was commoditize information. By being magically transformed into data, everything we know would be accessible to anyone with a computer, and "anyone" would eventually become "everyone."

This notion had some powerful advocates. Nicholas Negroponte, director of the MIT Media Lab and a contributor to the then-new *Wired* magazine, wrote in his 1995 book *Being Digital*, "The change from atoms to bits is irrevocable and unstoppable." He went on to cite breathtaking statistics, like the fact that the population of the Internet was growing at the rate of 10 per cent – a *month*. "Computing is not about computers any more," he wrote. "It is about living." That, many believed, would mean the end of the road for brands. If information were freely available to all, went their logic, then we would never need to buy anything on faith again. For them, information was the same as truth, and they relished a world in which the truth was not held hostage in a one-way, corporate-controlled media universe. Better still, this would bring the cost of marketing crashing to the ground. The Web would not only make information free, it would also allow entrepreneurs to compete as peers with big corporations. Not only would the truth be free, but so would good ideas. Ideas that consumers could find and sort out using nothing but the righteous shining light of data.

As is generally the case when it comes to the future, of course, nobody was right.

Most spectacularly wrong were the marketers. With blinding speed, computers and the Internet became absolutely normal. In no time at all, the web resembled a vast mall that, new as it was, seemed like it had always been there. That said, though, the corporate cow is an adaptable beast. Almost as quickly, corporations planted their flags on this *terra incognita*, and it soon seemed as if they had always been there, too. Less wrong, but more interestingly so, were the geeks and seers. That this phenomenon would be transformational and democratizing was obviously an accurate prediction. That this democratization would alter the nature of commerce was not. Yes, there was a lot more information and, yes, it was more accessible, but finding it turned out to be more work than most consumers could justify. Furthermore, those low barriers to entry were an invitation to every sort of carnival barker and scam artist imaginable. It wasn't always easy to distinguish the legitimate businesses, never mind the legitimate information. We used to be able to trust that a corporation had at least something of value to offer simply by its economic existence. On some level, we knew that you couldn't fake a skyscraper or a factory. Now, the only proxy for bricks and mortar was fame. The information age brought us empowerment, but it also brought us a lot of extra work and risk. For a lot of people a lot of the time, the solution to that problem would turn out to be brands after all.

One notably candid admission that brands were going to have a place in Internet utopia came from the most unlikely of people: Eric Schmidt, the CEO of Google. In October of 2008, speaking at the American Magazine Conference, the boss of the world's most trusted search engine said that the Internet was fast becoming a "cesspool" where false information thrives, and that a brand was a signal that content could be trusted. "Brands are the solution, not the problem," he said. "Brands are how you sort out the cesspool."

And you can't argue with Google.

The early days of the Web were not a democracy at all, in fact. They were just a giddy, well-intended anarchy. It was only with the arrival of brands that the consumer republic was finally born on the World Wide Web. Because now corporations had something extremely valuable to lose, in an environment over which they didn't have complete control. And because – and this is where the real Internet revolution was to happen, the one that even the geeks and seers didn't anticipate – it wasn't going to matter all that much what corporations said about their brands any more. What was going to matter was what *we* said about them.

———

The very same autumn that Eric Schmidt pronounced the Internet a cesspool, I had a chance to visit Google's office in New York City. I was invited there to participate in their Authors@Google series, and I naturally lunged at the chance to talk about my first book. Google, as a place of work, was everything you might imagine, unless you're just an unreconstructed skeptic. Everybody I met was young, crushingly bright, and switched on; every bit of architecture and design, coolly minimal, witty, and unassuming. Even the food in their cafeteria was spectacular, despite this not being one of the days when they invite a famous chef to cook for the company's *Wunderkinder* as they gaze out the lunchroom window at the Chrysler and Empire State buildings in the distance, monuments to a different sort of corporate hubris from a different sort of time.

But what struck me most about the place was the first thing you see as you approach the reception desk. Behind it, a huge video monitor broadcasts images from Google Earth, zooming in to a rooftop in some corner of the world, then back out to the planetary view, spinning and then zooming in again to another rooftop, endlessly poking and peering at our planet like a mischievous cat. And in front of the monitor, projected in spectral light from the ceiling to the floor, random words and phrases floated, utterly disconnected from one another, and changing constantly. Search queries. We were watching, before our eyes, what was on the world's mind.

My host later told me that, although these were real search queries, they were time delayed and had been cleansed of any inappropriate material, so technically I wasn't seeing exactly what was on the world's mind in *real* real time. Still, it made an impression. At first glance, you could be forgiven for feeling a little paranoid, seeing what the Internet knows about us. Reflecting on it a little longer, as I attempted to look comfortable in the slightly-too-minimalist lobby chair, I came to a different conclusion: The display in Google's lobby is not about us being under surveillance. Mostly, it's about us, for the very first time, talking back.

To understand why Internet search matters so much to the consumer republic, it's necessary to first understand the basics of how it works. We tend to think of search as rather magical, even as we take it for granted, but the essential mechanics of it are actually quite simple. Search is built on two fundamental tasks. First, a search engine "crawls" the Web on a regular basis, collecting every scrap of content it can find and using largely text-based cues to figure out how to categorize that content. That's called indexing. The result effectively works like an unimaginably vast grid of keywords someone might use to search for something, and the addresses of websites that contain anything resembling those words. The second thing a search engine does is match what it thinks you want with what it can find, in one way or another determining both the relevance and the relative credibility, or "rank," of the results. It's this second task that makes the difference between a good search engine and an extinct one.

In Google's case – and it is impossible not to pay special attention to Google's case – the secret sauce in its ranking process turns out, in a way, to be us. A critical factor in the way they rank search results is to look at clickstreams, the digital footprints we all leave wherever we go on the web. In the case of Google, they collect information on everything you see and read from the time you put in a search query until the end of your session. Add this to the recorded digital trails of billions of other Internet user sessions, and you have a formidable database of what we all collectively seem to think is worthwhile on the web and what isn't. All else being equal, a website that gets a lot of visitors who came from other sites that get a lot of visitors will rank more highly than one that, however brilliant, is a ghost town or has an exclusive audience of some kind. When you type "best riding lawn mower" into the box on Google's home page, the results you see first, aside from the paid or "sponsored" links, are determined by a mysterious formula that weighs how closely the content of the sites it can find resembles what you asked for (relevance) and, from among those sites, which ones have the most credibility based on the patterns of previous web users with roughly the same interests as yours.

Put another way, if the Internet really were a mall, the size and location of each store in it would be determined much more by shoppers than by architects and property developers. Which, if you ask me, sounds pretty darned democratic – revolutionary, even. If the Internet is going to be a key factor in our consuming behaviour – and it is – and if the choices search engines such as Google offer us are determined and validated by people *like* us rather than arbitrarily or by corporations who did nothing more than pay to be there, then could it not be said that the people have taken back the agora?

I posed this question to John Battelle, a journalist and co-founding editor of the magazine *Wired*, and today Chairman of Federated Media Publishing. Search – what it is, how it works, why it matters, and how it changes things – has been a passionate vocation for him virtually since it all began. In 2005, he wrote a book entitled *The Search: How Google and Its Rivals Rewrote the Rules of Business and Transformed Our Culture*. As one reviewer of that book succinctly put it, "Nobody, and I mean nobody, has thought longer, harder or smarter about Google and the search business." If Google and its ilk were the soul and guardians of democracy in the modern marketplace, he'd probably know about it.

As with most things revolutionary, the answer turns out not to be quite that simple. "Search," he told me, "*is* democratizing. But I couldn't say with confidence today that it's a democracy." It turns out that there is a lot going on behind that innocent-looking white screen full of blue hyperlinks. Let's start with the bad news.

First, it's important to remember that a vast amount of the information collected when a search engine crawls the web today is commercial. It wasn't always so. In the beginning, search was populist, if not necessarily democratic, because a large proportion of the web's content was created by amateurs. Search for the "best riding lawn mower" a decade ago, and much of what you would find would be the writings of "riding mower-obsessed people," says Battelle. "The data set came from freaks. Search *was* democratic in that the web was not operated by an oligarchy of John Deere and Toro and Sears." It still isn't today, but the odds of a search returning content that amounts to advertising or is at least commercially motivated are much higher. The gravitational pull of brand familiarity is going to perpetuate that. The simple fact that we keep clicking on brands as a way of "sorting out the cesspool" actually strengthens the position of those brands even in an environment as supposedly neutral as an Internet search engine.

Second, corporations are furiously gaming the system to improve their profiles in search results. Search Engine Optimization (SEO) is a fully realized profession in the marketing communications business today, and it employs a variety of tools to push a site's rank higher on a search results page. Some SEO is arguably valuable to the user, in that the content of a site gets massaged to more closely match the kinds of information its data says most people look for; other practices have been murkier and more manipulative, and sometimes even fraudulent. Either way, none of it serves the purpose of the search engine, whose business depends on its own credibility as an honest broker of democratically validated information. What we see on the results page of a search seems to have all the earnest helpfulness of a librarian with an armload of books. Behind the screen, though, "It's an arms race between search engines and corporations," as Battelle put it. The ever-adaptive corporate cow relentlessly tries to find a hole in the fence, while the search engine tirelessly fights to preserve the neutrality on which its business is based.

Speaking of which – and third – search engines like Google *are* in business, and that business is advertising. Google, too, is a cow. The money it, and companies like it, earns, it earns by selling the opportunity to advertise to us in one way or another, and that money comes from the corporations who want to sell us lawn mowers. I really believe that Google is crystal clear in its collective cyber-mind that agnostic search results are sacred to their business model. But I also believe that Google needs to help those corporations find us in order to make money, and so, even as they're fully engaged in an "arms race" with them, they'll always be at the same time searching for the boundaries of legitimacy. Which means that, for us, as Thomas Jefferson might have put it, the price of democratic Internet search will be eternal vigilance.

And yet.

Search, more than any other artifact of the Internet age, has absolutely transformed the relationship between corporations and marketplaces because, as Battelle forcefully put it, "now, [corporations] have to join the conversation." For the first time ever, as search technology matured, corporations could not control everything that was said and heard about their brands in the agora, nor could they safely stand idle while it was being said. In order to make sure that their brands had a fighting chance, marketers were forced to engage. At best, to be silent would be to risk slipping off the radar, and at worst it would risk a brand's reputation being defined entirely by its enemies, whose ruminations might be all a search could find. Not to listen, meanwhile, would be the approximate corporate equivalent of clapping your hands on your ears, closing your eyes, and shouting "la la la la" – while standing on a train track. And, for corporations, this would be the worst part: Managing a brand's reputation would never again be a matter of creating an annual marketing plan, deploying it, and waiting for the results. The battle for hearts, minds, and wallets would be conducted daily, hourly, by the minute, in real time, and the terms of engagement would be dictated at least partly by the marketplace. By us. By what's on our minds. Brands would have to learn how to react as well as how to act, and to listen as well as to talk. They would have to look us in the eye. With bovine reluctance, most of them are now trying to learn to do just that.

Before the Internet, before search, brands had always been like smug little monarchies, dispensing persuasion and amusement from their remote palaces without resistance from a passive populace. Now, the marketplace is like an election campaign. A rough-and-tumble election campaign that never, ever ends.

———

"ok headed to grant park!" tweeted Rahaf Harfoush, in what is surely the most understated post in Twitter's short history. It was just before 10:00 p.m. on November 4, 2008, and she was on her way from a Chicago office building to the city's historic gathering place to hear her boss accept the job of President of the United States.

Rahaf Harfoush is, as I write this, Associate Director of the Global Redesign Initiative at the World Economic Forum in Geneva, and a respected new media strategist. The young, unassuming, and whip-smart consultant found her calling early. When she was barely out of school, she worked as a research coordinator with author Don Tapscott on two books dealing

with the socially transformative power of technology –
Wikinomics: How Mass Collaboration Changes Everything and
Grown Up Digital: The Rise of the Net Generation. In 2008,
seeing the Presidential election in the United States as a turning
point for the world, she presented her credentials as a volunteer
to Barack Obama's New Media Team at the campaign's Chicago
headquarters and was invited to join the cause. For the next
three months, Harfoush was immersed in a process that would
make history in more ways than just the obvious ones. In one,
stunningly sudden moment, propelled by the mother of all
branding challenges, social media – technology platforms like
Facebook and Twitter – went from being widely regarded in the
marketing world as irrelevant diversions to being crucial obses-
sions. Given the campaign's stunning demonstration of what
social media can do, the bleeding economy that made conventional media coincidentally unaffordable for many corporations
at the time, and the breathtaking growth in the number of consumers using these new communications channels, the corporate
world pounced on any chance to meet the people and get their
brands elected.

That's how the case study of America's first Internet President
is widely reported. Even Rahaf Harfoush's own book chronicling the campaign, *Yes We Did: An Inside Look at How Social
Media Built the Obama Brand*, sets out to share its lessons so
as to inspire marketers to join the conversation (the same word,
you'll recall, that John Battelle used to describe the effect of
Internet search on commerce; the same immensely significant
word, in fact, that everybody who lives and breathes the social
web uses). But what some of those readers might miss in their
zeal to learn the secrets of this new craft, and what many corporations didn't count on when they began to "join

the conversation," is the bargain they strike when they engage consumers in such an intimate, human way. Facebook is not the Super Bowl. This channel goes both ways, all the time. And everyone can hear what's being said. By wading into the universe of social media, a brand invites its constituency to help shape it. That's the deal. The Obama campaign accepted this risk more knowingly than, say, United Airlines obviously did, and actually invited people into the process of setting its policy agenda. But even they were not entirely prepared for what that invitation can mean.

When I asked her for an example, Rahaf Harfoush answered without hesitation: FISA. The acronym stands for Foreign Intelligence Surveillance Act, a piece of legislation dating back to 1978. Its purpose was to govern the process of covertly gathering information on the activities of foreign countries and individuals where they might affect the security of the United States. In 2008, the Bush government proposed a set of amendments to the Act, including several contentious provisions. One expanded the government's power to spy on citizens' private communications. Another gave telecommunications companies immunity from being sued by their customers for assisting with such spying, whether it had occurred in the past or would occur in the future. The Senator from Illinois had initially taken a firm position against the proposed changes to FISA, but as these things sometimes go in political life, Obama changed that position in the summer of 2008, ultimately supporting the amendments. In old-fashioned politics, his about-face might have gone altogether unnoticed, or perhaps enjoyed a brief, grumpy moment in the journalistic spotlight before being eclipsed by the next issue. In new-fashioned politics, Barack Obama wasn't going to get away with it quite that easily.

The centrepiece of the Obama campaign's new media strategy was a website called *my.barackobama.com* (referred to by campaigners as MyBO). This Facebook-style community site for volunteers and supporters of the campaign was created, in fact, by Facebook co-founder Chris Hughes. It was designed to allow people to connect with one another, share information, organize events, raise funds, and, significantly, form groups in order to speak and be heard. The candidate used it as a channel through which to encourage and inspire his supporters, and they in turn used it as a way to tell him what was on their minds. Before the FISA issue came along, this channel had been a powerful asset to the campaign, giving the candidate and his team constructive campaign input from the grassroots level, and the sort of praise and encouragement one might expect from a partisan community. The FISA controversy, though, showed that this intimate connectedness was a double-edged sword.

In short order following Obama's decision to change his position on the FISA amendments, a new group was formed by members on MyBO, dedicated to pressuring the Senator to change his mind. Gathering steam quickly, it was soon one of the largest groups that had yet been formed on the site – more than 22,000 members at its peak – and those members were more direct than deferential. "If you want my support, you will have to stand up for the rule of law and not further undermining [sic] our constitution," wrote one. "You should not take for granted that we will support you [with our money]." In the end, rather than change his mind, the Senator defended his decision to support the amendments. He issued a direct statement to the MyBO group, and his policy team took the unprecedented step of conducting real-time Q&A sessions with group members to hear their concerns personally rather than filtered by polls or the media. And that's the point: he had to listen, and he had to defend his decision.

In fact, as the controversy unfolded, two radical new dynamics evolved that are quickly becoming the new normal in the marketing world. One of them had to do with accountability. Obama was forced to swiftly and directly justify his decision in the very same two-way forums that members of the group had used to criticize his decision, rather than from a media pulpit. The channel his team had created brought with it a special and immediate kind of accountability. As one political blogger wrote, "The fact is, we're all entering completely new territory here. There have always been efforts to influence political candidates to take or change positions during a campaign (or afterward), but we've never before had a national campaign create an open platform for mobilizing supporters and then seen a salient chunk of those supporters openly use that platform to challenge the candidate on a policy position." Support, in other words, was constantly provisional, and the candidate was going to have to earn it every day.

The second dynamic had to do with transparency. Unlike in the days when politicians solved policy problems in smoky back rooms, this dialogue itself became a story, amplifying the issue and subjecting it to more public scrutiny. The *New York Times* and other news outlets covered the "intense backlash" from Obama's supporters as ardently as they would have the original issue. Conversation begat conversation, and all of it was on the record. If it hadn't been clear before, it was certainly clear now: The Obama brand did not exclusively belong to Barack Obama and his campaign team. Its meaning, its credibility, and its fate rested ultimately in the hands of the people who had chosen – provisionally – to believe in it.

Rahaf Harfoush's book chronicling the campaign resonates with the argument that brands are no longer little monarchies but instead have become rowdy republics. Before the social web, she told me, a politician "didn't have to explain himself to anybody. He got elected, and we sent him off to government trusting that he would represent our interests. Now, representation isn't enough." With a passion and language that echoes John Battelle's, she says that the transformation of media from one-way broadcast into two-way conversation is both irrevocable and "challenges the entire philosophy of the [political] system." She recalls a cautionary piece of wisdom that routinely made the rounds of Obama's New Media Team when they reflected on what they were doing. It was widely attributed by the team, in fact, to Obama himself. Describing the challenging bargain of social media engagement, the Senator from Illinois said, "It's like having an angry tiger by the tail."

Very quickly, and just as irrevocably, the same thing is happening to the brands in our marketplaces. And we are the tiger.

I don't think the consumer tiger is always angry, mind you, but neither do I think it's infallible. Like any young democracy, the consumer republic can be a bit chaotic and the conversation can be dominated by people whose volubility shouldn't be confused with a licence to represent us all. The social web has always been and remains a problematic resource if you're looking for that elusive perfect riding mower. It's hard to judge the credibility of a lot of the information you find out there, as Google's Schmidt so eloquently observed. And it's true that the most vocal contributors to that body of information are often the most unhappy and temperamental, and sometimes still the looniest. For every solid, objective source of information about brands and their products on the web, there are a hundred or a thousand or ten thousand that are contaminated by a hidden agenda of one kind or another. All of that will change and get better with time, and all the more quickly if everyone joins the conversation. One day, surely, this democracy will grow up and the corporations who sell us branded products will have as much legitimate public accountability for keeping their promises as, say, an eBay seller. Or an aspiring President of the United States.

While we wait for that day, the greater truth about the social web remains that, as with our system of government, it is its very existence that should give us the most hope. The fact that we're talking about brands in public forums, however imperfectly and lopsidedly, is institutionalizing the need for corporations to listen. As both Battelle and Harfoush emphatically told me, corporations now have no choice. So it's not surprising that the number of companies now actively monitoring Facebook and Twitter to see what we're saying about them is in the many thousands already. The number is growing all the time, as is the sophistication of their listening tools. Months after my interview with John Battelle, my nearly new John Deere garden tractor actually broke down mid-lawn. I complained about it – idly – on Twitter, which precipitated a stealthy visit to my blog by someone at Deere within two hours of my post. In this case, thanks to my own web analytics, the surveillance was satisfyingly mutual. It was satisfying to know they'd heard this lone blogger, even if no offer of intervention was immediately forthcoming. It was satisfying to know that, even if only briefly, I'd made them nervous.

Where surveillance had been hit-and-miss during the social media's early days, now some big names in consumer research and business analytics are taking it very seriously. In May of 2010, for example, no less a titan than IBM presented the corporate herd with a new way to monitor the entire social web for brand sentiment, and to do it so sensitively that they could interpret relevant slang and even emoticons. With vaguely Orwellian irony, the good people at IBM promised "true customer intimacy." Their new surveillance tool aimed to leave no stone unturned in the effort to keep track of how we're feeling about the brands we choose . . . or don't.

IBM had certainly identified a ripe market. As 2009 drew to a close, almost 80 per cent of the Fortune Global 100 corporate cows had already become directly engaged in social media in one or more forms, a quantum leap from the year before Obama's historic speech in Grant Park. Most aren't only listening; they're talking, too. Of the corporations that use Twitter, for example, more than 80 per cent are tweeting at least weekly, and just less than half of those are doing so in response to people who had something to say to them. Many of those same corporations are frantically trying to reorganize the very structures of their marketing, public relations, and customer service functions. They are inventing new jobs to deal with the new reality that their brands are going to depend not on the occasional grand gesture but on millions and millions of little public exchanges. They're fast learning that, on the social web, silence both speaks loudly and remains on the record. Brands, as John Battelle put it during an exchange on Twitter, are platforms now, and marketers had better start thinking of themselves as publishers if they want any influence over their reputations. I have never seen anything make the marketing world more nervous – and attentive – than the simple fact that the web has become a social gathering place.

But let's not get too comfortable. Knowing this alone isn't enough to build a consumer republic. Corporations are madly trying to adapt to the changes brought about by social media not so much because of what they have meant so far, but because of what they fear these changes will mean in the future. So far, people who had the same sort of passion as the "freaks" who built the original web have set the pattern for activism on the social web. The corporate cow is operating on the assumption that we know how much power we have, that we're willing to use it, and that more and more of us are on the way, pitchforks and torches in hand. Sweating in peacetime so as to bleed less in the coming revolutionary war, they're trying to stockpile goodwill and manage the narratives of their brands on the Internet against the day when eye-to-eye dialogue is how a brand must be built and defended. They have no choice.

But neither do we. Engagement here, in the wide-open, two-way, transparent marketplace, has got to be as essential to the way we do business as it is for them. Our silence, too, would speak loudly. It would sound, in fact, like endorsement. And it, too, would remain forever on the record.

———

I live part of my time near a very small town about ninety minutes north of Toronto. Around here, as they say in small towns everywhere, everybody knows everybody. That kind of social intimacy breeds some interesting cultural dynamics, especially when it comes to one's reputation. It starts, of course, with the fact that you have one at all. In a small town, you're never anonymous. People wave at the sight of your truck, because they know it's yours. They gossip about you, because stories are currency in small communities. And while they may be very forgiving – you have to be in order to make a community work – they don't forget. Whether you're a plumber or a pharmacist or a weekender in shiny Hunter boots, every observable thing you do, say, drive, and wear accretes to your reputation, and the effect of that reputation is brought to bear on every contact you have with your fellow citizens, including the commercial ones. As a city person, if you're not careful, you can fall into the trap of thinking your conduct doesn't matter. Until, that is, you need that plumber. So you have to be decent. You can't burn bridges. And, again as in every rural community everywhere, you can't ever get too full of yourself.

For brands on the Internet, this is increasingly what life is like. Not only can't they control everything that's said about them any more, but they can't even decide when they want to be observed and when they don't. They're on stage all the time. Every story, and the bad more so than the good, spreads like a grass fire and remains archived, seemingly forever, somewhere on-line. Faced with that reality, it's delightful and ironic to see that brands are finding themselves subject to forces that are cousin to Liz Suhay's social-emotional influence phenomenon. While brands themselves don't form a coherent community, their behaviour and stated beliefs are every bit as driven by the desire to avoid shame and seek pride as Suhay argues yours and mine are. It's early days, of course. This town is still pretty small, and most brands could still flee back to the status quo if they had to, for a while at least. But the fact is that the Internet didn't create anything new where branded marketing is concerned. What it did was tear down barricades that kept us from dealing with those brands eye to eye, the way people did before there were any "media" at all. Now, we can truly judge the characters of the brands we interact with. Now, we can contribute directly to their reputations. Now, in a very real sense, they belong to us.

What's essential and urgent is that we realize it. Look too closely at the evolution of consumerism on the Internet, and you see frantic creativity and an incomprehensible pace of mutation and adaptation. With more than half of North American Internet users having less than a decade of experience on-line, the subject seems either to deserve several speculative books of its own or to be too unsettled to draw any conclusions on at all. Stand far enough back from the teeming cesspool, though, and what you see is altogether simpler and more fundamental to our way of life. For a citizen of the consumer republic, this is the commons, the forum. To be a citizen of the consumer republic, without question, you have to be a citizen of the Internet.

CHAPTER TEN

BEND IT LIKE BUFFETT

The first time you set foot on Wall Street, it can surprise
you.

For example, it's small. Less than a half-mile long, it
starts at a TD Bank branch at Broadway and veers southeast
toward the East River, ending without fanfare just past Starbucks.
It's also narrow – the northwestern end is actually a pedestrian
mall, now, thanks to security worries – and not especially showy,
architecturally speaking. If the Masters of the Universe are really
here, they're keeping a low profile. All you're likely to see is a
bunch of office workers in shirtsleeves, poking away at their
BlackBerrys while they wait their turn for a kebab from a street
vendor, punctuated by the occasional tourist or over-caffeinated
cop. In fact, the bronze sculpture of the raging bovine that we
all associate with New York's financial district isn't even here.
For a neighbourhood that's watched so intently by the whole
world, Wall Street is, in the flesh, a pretty unremarkable and
human-scale place.

And then there is the statue in front of Federal Hall near
the corner of Wall and Nassau Streets. It's not a monument to

some swashbuckling plutocrat from capitalism's storied past; it is a statue of George Washington. As it happens, this is the site of his swearing in as the first President of the United States in 1789. It is also the place where the United States Bill of Rights was ratified into law not long afterward. Democracy and commerce, in other words, turn out to have arrived in the New World at almost exactly the same moment in almost exactly the same spot. Their fates inextricably linked, they have been keeping a wary eye on each other ever since.

Of all the signals that we, the people, send to the corporate world, the way we invest our money is both the most direct and the most muted. An ugly running shoe, a foul-tasting chewing gum, or a hideous couch can all be put on sale. A dimwitted advertising campaign can be taken off the air, a quality problem can be fixed, and a pricing error can be corrected with a few keystrokes. But the value of a stock is what it is, at least until the next trading session starts. There is scarcely a more direct line to the leadership of a publicly owned company, scarcely a more certain way to hit a CEO right where he lives, than to sell a company's stock because you don't believe in it. At the same time, though, it's equally true that our voices seem very small in that world. Most of us might invest in what amounts to a handful of shares of any given company when compared to what the truly rich can afford. And even the richest investors' voices are drowned out by the mighty institutional investors that actually move markets. Indeed, our most recent financial mess hardly involved the ordinary citizens at all, unless you count the ones who borrowed too much money to buy too much real estate. Like all those kebab-munching Masters of the Universe who walk right past George Washington every day without a glance upward, capitalism, it sometimes seems, has almost completely detached itself from the life of the ordinary person.

"Almost" is the operative word, here. What happens on the world's Wall Streets is still important to the citizen of the consumer republic. It's important in the obvious sense that about 50 per cent of all North Americans are investors in equities, and many more of us – through pension funds and insurance policies – are indirectly in the same boat. Our money still talks. It's also important in the less obvious sense that the markets are keeping an account for us of the value created by the companies with which we do business. As a marketing professor of mine was fond of brutally putting it, "The sole purpose of a corporation is to make money for its shareholders. Everything else it does is a means to that end." If there's any truth in it, then the scoreboard is here, just up the street from Starbucks, across from a falafel stand. It begs the question of whether the way money is made on Wall Street encourages the kind of corporate behaviour we want, or whether as investors we are effectively and unwittingly compelled to cheer them on in their effort to become exactly the kinds of companies we hate the most as consumers.

———

This chapter isn't even a little bit about how to make money in the markets – that's a matter for you and your financial advisor to discuss. No, this chapter is about the connection – whether one exists, and if it does, its nature – between branded marketing as the face of capitalism and the machinery behind it. Are we still having the same kind of conversation when we vote our money on a corporation's shares rather than on its products?

Perhaps more fundamentally, can our vision of a consumer republic even mesh with the machinery of capitalism? Or is the idea of "slow consumerism" and of making corporations accountable through the brands they sell just a way to shoot ourselves in the collective foot?

Stock markets are, in effect, a giant meta-cow. Down on Wall Street, the Masters of the Universe are completely oblivious to the differences among laundry detergents or running shoes or, for that matter, the difference between a running shoe and a pork belly. They do what works, and what works is defined simply and purely as making money. Buying and selling shares in publicly owned companies is a staple way of doing this, and among the various distinctions the pros apply to describe the investors they represent and the stocks they choose, one of the most broadly used is the one between "growth" and "value." The terms technically refer to styles of investing, but it's hard not to see them as symbols of a basic philosophical divide in the consumer republic, one with closer ties to the theme of brands and accountability than you might imagine. Here's what I mean.

A growth investor is someone who chooses stocks on the basis of the rate at which those companies are growing, and likely to continue growing. This investor will pay much less attention to the price of a stock as it relates to how a company is run, what it sells, and what it owns and earns, and much more to how fast that company is growing relative to the market overall. In more extreme cases, a growth investor will disregard the former entirely and look at the rate of growth alone. In the most extreme cases, they'll place their bets not even on the basis of how fast that company is growing but on the basis of how fast *other* investors *believe* it will grow in the future. These investors frequently don't even plan to hold on to the stock they buy. Growth investing turns the stock market into something more akin to off-track betting than to public ownership. Stocks are the racehorses and every trading day is a new race. Too much of this kind of investing eventually abstracts stocks completely from the companies behind them. What happens then is called a "bubble," and it never ends well.

To bet on growth is to encourage it, so, in boom times, this investment philosophy encourages corporate builders, the entrepreneurs with the vision and imagination to create an asset out of thin air. Growth is the romance of the markets, the worship of possibility. But often (though thankfully not always), the companies that attract this kind of investor are, themselves, obsessed with their stock price rather than creative capitalism. Their CEOs are, effectively, paid to make it go up, and they along with senior managers can be further encouraged by the granting of options to purchase shares in the future at a price that's fixed today. Simply put, these people can buy and then resell shares in their employer's company at a personal profit, so long as the price of those shares rises between the time they received the options and the time they exercised them. I've worked with executive-level marketing people who actually tracked their stock price daily and even hourly on their smartphones, and would even interrupt a meeting to call out a significant move. As a branding guy, it left me with no doubt as to what really mattered to those marketers. And very often it can even transform the purpose of a corporation from the creation of value to the creation of the *appearance* of value and the promise of more to come. When growth becomes a corporate obsession, strangely, the consumer – her interest, her trust, her satisfaction – can leave the equation entirely.

The value investor is a different sort of animal, and on the surface a more conservative one. This investor chooses stock not on the basis of whether the market will raise its price in the future, but on the basis of the difference between that company's stock price and what it might really be worth ("worth" meaning, for example, that its assets are undervalued somehow, or that it is capable of generating a reliable income for its shareholders even if it's not growing in size). If stocks were houses, the growth investor would be betting that the neighbourhood is going to move upscale, and the value investor would be betting that the house is solid and will deliver shelter and comfort for a long time while providing a hedge against inflation. One is an entrepreneur, and the other is a saver.

The companies whose stocks are considered "value" stocks aren't vice-free as marketers, either. They sometimes tend to be more risk-averse, less agile at or capable of adapting to changes in the marketplace, and at worst even arrogantly closed-minded. Nevertheless, they share one quality that a citizen of the consumer republic can respect: a reverence for economic sustainability. Companies that earn the "value" badge are deeply concerned with being able to keep doing what they are doing, namely doing what works, over and over again, year after year, forever.

In my experience, there are essentially three styles of corporate marketing. There are what I'll call the "farmers," who worry every day about whether their land can continue to produce and whether they planted the right crop. Packaged goods companies tend to fit this description. They know they need to win you over again with each weekly grocery run. Then there are what I'll call the "loggers," who busy themselves exploiting their marketplaces and figuring that they can reverse the damage they've done by reforesting it later. A lot of technology and fashion companies are like loggers. They know that each product cycle will be short and intense, but that everything they sell will eventually be obsolete and they'll have to earn your trust all over again. Finally, there are what I'll call the "miners," who keep digging until all the gold is gone and then move on to start a new hole. From a branding perspective, pharmaceutical companies can be like this, given their brands' reputations are rarely built to last past the limit of their patent protection.

Value investors are "slow capitalists," and they tend to bet their money on the farmers of capitalism. And so it makes some kind of sense that their king makes his home a long way from Wall Street, in relatively bucolic Omaha, Nebraska.

——

If we want to understand the potential of public ownership in the capitalist system, Warren Buffett seems like a good place to start. He is defensibly the world's most successful investor, and as a consequence, one of its richest inhabitants. In the former capacity, his Berkshire Hathaway Inc. has averaged annual growth in its book value of 20.3 per cent per year over more than four decades. In the latter capacity, he regularly vies with the likes of Bill Gates for a position among the top three or so (in 2010, he was in third place). Inside the world of investing, Buffett is an endless focus of awe and controversy, his every word carefully studied and parsed; outside in the real world, he is capitalism's poster child, cheerfully pragmatic, endlessly quotable, an affable uncle to our faith in the system. If there's a right way to play this game, Warren Buffett is as close as anyone to knowing what it is. And he is a value investor of the very highest order. That alone, given his success, is a persuasive argument that what makes a successful capitalist is not wholly at odds with what makes a good citizen of the consumer republic.

Dig a little deeper, though, and it gets better. There is more here than a simple correlation between investing in conservatively run companies and consistently making a lot of money. On closer examination, the world's most successful investor buys companies in the same way that we ought to be buying home appliances and snow tires, and runs his business not much differently than we ought to be running our lives. Accept for a minute this remarkable example of one investor as proof that (a) patience, reasonable expectations, and a flinty eye for value need not destroy our collective way of life any more than they do our individual ones, and (b) these qualities might, in fact, provide a better path to prosperity than greed ever would on its best day. Warren Buffett, with his personal net worth of $47 billion dollars, famous frugality, and tidy, grey three-bedroom stucco house in the centre of Omaha, provides us with compelling evidence that this whole consumer republic thing might just work, and that the secret is *there is no secret*. For starters, Warren Buffett buys brands.

It's the most striking thing about Berkshire Hathaway's portfolio, so much so that it would probably raise your eyebrows even if the subject didn't interest you. Of the forty common stock positions Buffett's holding company held at the time of this writing, easily three-quarters were corporations that made branded products you and I might buy. Nor were these obscure or minor players. Companies like Procter & Gamble, Johnson & Johnson, Nestlé, and Kraft fill our shopping carts weekly. Routine trips to Home Depot, Lowes, and Costco are part of life for millions of families. He owns shares in companies that insure our cars and fill their gas tanks, put shoes on our feet and cash in our wallets (from our own chequing accounts, mind you). And of the companies where his stake is large, large enough to ensure that CEOs will take his phone calls, every one is not only a household name but a titan in its category: Coca-Cola (the world's most valuable brand), Procter & Gamble (the consumer products giant that markets Tide, Dawn, Crest, Olay, Pampers, Head and Shoulders, Pringles, Duracell, and Gillette), Anheuser-Busch (Budweiser, Michelob, and Busch), American Express, the Washington Post Company (a media conglomerate), and M&T Bank (a commercial bank with 750 branches in the northeastern United States). In Warren Buffett's shopping cart, there is a noticeable lack of generic-ness.

What's the attraction? Surely the world's most successful investor has something more adventurous in his bag of tricks than dandruff shampoo. Why would he choose to own companies that make a few cents every time we brush our teeth or apply deodorant when he could be making a villainous fortune digging minerals out of the ground or playing Wall Street games with shadowy corporate giants that do their work far from the glare of the mall? Well, for one thing, brands happen to make money. According to one researcher, publicly owned companies that invest in marketing their brands have outperformed the S&P 500 by four hundred basis points a year, every year since 1997. Of those companies, the top 20 per cent beat the market by 17 per cent a year. For Buffett, the answer also seems to have a lot to do with predictability. He likes companies that have "demonstrated consistent earning power." Companies that have sold things to us for many years have that. They earn their money every week rather than in one or two high-stakes, military-procurement-sized deals a year. They have long histories. They make or do things we generally think we need, so demand is stable. And by being branded as well as established companies, he can assume they enjoy a sustainable competitive advantage and are motivated to preserve it. In other words, they are farms. If they're well run, they'll produce year after year, bushel after reliable bushel of cash, all based on the presumption that people like you and me are endorsing the value of their products.

Which is really the point. It's nice to see the world's third-richest man prosper by buying sensibly rather than foolishly; it provides us with a lovely metaphor for the way we should behave at the mall and some symbolic encouragement that it pays to do so. But the real news, here, is that the fortunes of the world's third-richest man are very much in our hands. The value in the brands he invests in is put there by consumers, and the corporations behind them are obsessively paying attention to what we think and do, because it's the only way they can make money and apparently the only way they can sustain their share prices. The research report I quoted earlier summarized the growing democracy of the markets with this blunt warning: "A company's brand can be one of the few true competitive advantages remaining in modern industry."

That assessment is borne out convincingly by an annual study of corporate reputations conducted by the research firm Harris Interactive. The study looks at Americans' general regard for the corporate world, ranks highly visible corporations in terms of their esteem for each one, and then goes deeper to see whether that esteem actually leads to people trusting those companies with their money. To nobody's surprise, it does. Of the fourteen brands from whom 29,000-odd Americans said they would "definitely" buy products in the future, nine were also among the fifteen corporate brands whose reputations achieved a rating of "Excellent" in the same study. And guess what? The stocks of seven of those nine corporations just happen to be in Warren Buffett's portfolio. That's major overlap. It seems to add weight to the argument that a corporation that gets big and a brand that gets famous by satisfying its customers rather than by taking advantage of them is a pretty good investment. Value actually does beget value. And, again, it's we, in the end, who decide through the brands we choose what that value will be. Warren Buffett, in other words, trusts whomever we trust. Accountability is apparently not antithetical to successful capitalism – at least, not as long as we're willing to be picky about what we buy.

Oh, and in case you were wondering which corporation had the best reputation of all in the Harris study, well, that would be Berkshire Hathaway. The leading brand of capitalism may not be on anything we can buy at the mall, but that doesn't mean we don't recognize value when we see it.

———

In 1983, Warren Buffett put pen to paper to "set down 13 owner-related business principles, that [he] thought would help new shareholders understand [Berkshire's] managerial approach." The principles make an appearance, unchanged, every year in the company's annual report, which Buffett thinks "is appropriate for 'principles.'" Written in his own voice, as most of the annual report is, the principles and their rationales are frank, chatty, and reassuringly pragmatic. The most dominant theme in the declarations is accountability. "Most of our directors have a major portion of their net worth invested in the company," he writes in one instance. "We eat our own cooking . . . when

I do something dumb, I want you to be able to derive some solace from the fact that my financial suffering is proportional to yours." (Well, with $47 billion, Buffett may have a little more financial runway than most, but the sentiment is noble all the same.) Berkshire Hathaway also seems to put its money where its mouth is, even when it comes to the companies whose shares they own. "As owners of, say, Coca-Cola or American Express shares," their leader says, "we think of Berkshire Hathaway as being a non-managing partner."

So he is. For better or worse, Buffett's attachment to his investments is personal. His view of investment bankers is reportedly that they are "useless, self-serving windbags," whereas he is famously available as an advisor to the CEOs of companies in which he has a significant stake. There is a lot to admire about that attitude, at least in principle. Like Stephanie Nolen and her iPod, Buffett believes in being connected to where his money comes from and in taking some responsibility for it. In fact, at the company's annual meeting, Berkshire Hathaway rents 194,000 square feet of space adjacent to the meeting hall, where shareholders can browse through and buy products made by the companies Berkshire Hathaway has invested in. A stunt, perhaps, or maybe a symbolic reminder of the firm's belief that only real commerce creates legitimate wealth. Whatever it may be, it illustrates how Buffett doesn't turn a blind eye toward the machine that creates his wealth or avoid the truth about how (this would cause him some grief in the spring of 2010, when he publicly and unpopularly defended his investment in Goldman Sachs). We could well do the same, whether it's with our own investments or our choice of patio furniture.

By being so personal about it, it seems all but inevitable that Buffett's own business principles should infect the companies he invests in. He abhors debt, for example. He places a premium on competent management over fancy business models. He doesn't invest in products or business models he doesn't understand. And he thinks CEOs should have some skin in the game. In the 2009 Berkshire Hathaway annual report, he wrote of financial institutions, "The CEOs and directors of the failed companies, however, have largely gone unscathed. Their fortunes may have been diminished by the disasters they oversaw, but they still live in grand style." He railed, "[They] have long benefitted from oversized financial carrots; some *meaningful* sticks [italics his] now need to be part of their employment picture as well."

You can draw your own conclusions about whether this is a great investment strategy, but, again, $47 billion suggests it sure isn't a bad one. And, again, Berkshire Hathaway isn't really the point anyway. This is the point: just as when you shop, you can invest according to your ethics and your principles, you can face and connect with the companies in which you choose to have a stake, and you can be an activist about their accountability, and apparently – thanks in part to the power of brands – none of this needs to stand in the way of getting what you want.

——

"Charlie [Vice Chairman Munger] and I avoid businesses whose futures we can't evaluate, no matter how exciting their products may be," wrote Buffett in his 2009 letter to shareholders. "Future projections are of no interest to us," he said in the Acquisition Criteria section later in the same document. It's a Warren Buffett mantra. Hope is dangerous.

As consumers, hope makes us do things we regret more times than not. We buy a car with payments a little bigger than we can really afford, betting that our incomes will somehow improve before too many lean months go by. We buy a house that's fancier or larger than we can really use, betting that the value of the property will magically rise and turn our negative net worths into positive ones. Like that bourgeois wage slave Tony Soprano, we voluntarily put ourselves on these treadmills, and our excuse for doing it is the hope that life will improve and retroactively make sense of the bets we placed. So it is with the markets. Shares can trade in a stock that is priced on the basis of dozens or even, in the case of a bubble like the dot com frenzy of the late 1990s, hundreds of times what that company is earning in profits annually at that moment, and people will keep buying. Why? If we accept that the intention of investors is to make a profit for themselves, there are really only two possible reasons: they hope that the company they invested in will grow at a parabolic rate and thus bring their purchase price down to a more reasonable multiple of its earnings, or they hope that there are legions of investors out there who are even more arrogantly optimistic than they are and who will take the shares off their hands at an even higher price before reason prevails. From seventeenth-century tulip futures to twenty-first-century mortgage-backed securities, practically every calamity in the history of institutionalized investing has been propelled by the triumph of hope over common sense.

That's a choice that everyone is free to make, of course, just as with lottery tickets, casinos, and parking meters. Without a doubt, some people do win impressively, when they make it. But most of the time it is the plodding tortoise and not the manic hare who gets to the finish line in life, and the fact that no investment guru has yet devised a formula for massively outperforming the market indexes in a sustainable way seems like proof that hope alone, at least when it comes to our money, is the longest of long shots. That doesn't seem to be how the world's most successful investor operates. He seems to understand that the market for soft drinks, running shoes, and plumbing fixtures is going to be inevitably tied to the number of bellies, feet, and bathrooms in the world, and that those numbers will grow at a steady and predictable pace, a pace unlikely to much exceed that of human reproduction. It's a very grounded point of view, and though it's dressed up in the folksy patois that is Warren Buffett's personal brand, it has its basis in the more practical reality that the only certain and sustainable way to make money in this world is by making things that people value.

In our economic lives, hope is kind of like chocolate cake: a sweet and happy diversion essential to a healthy spirit but fatal if you subsist on it. Here in the consumer republic, there are two compelling arguments for keeping the portions small.

The first is that hope invites exploitation. Whether you're considering the purchase of a penny stock or a jar of anti-wrinkle cream, when you face a marketplace with the irrational certainty that you can beat the universe at its own game, there will be people who see you as easy money. Like magnets, hopeful consumers and cynical opportunists are forcefully attracted to one another, and it's no accident. By now, it's well understood that the economic meltdown of the past few years had its roots in hopeful consumers betting on the real estate bubble, preyed upon by cynical lenders and morally disengaged Wall Street types. That's only the latest and grandest episode in a long history of investment chicanery. But it happens at the mall, too. Until the 1990s, when the idea of status was dismantled by Dr. McCracken's tribal teenagers, "aspiration" was the magic bullet for all sorts of branded marketing. Corporations and their advertising agencies consciously presented the products they sold as totems of our better selves. It was, for the most part, a consensual vanity; consumers were happily complicit in the wide-shouldered '80s dream of status and affluence. In the words of one legendary ad man, ads and brands were "statements of what you [thought] life should be about." But at the margins, then and now, there were plenty of marketers with less to lose who crossed the line from dream to false promise. In the skin cream business, marketers like that called what they sold "hope in a jar." They knew what they were doing. When hope alone is what works, corporations can behave badly.

The second has to do with a little trick that our minds play on us when we overindulge in baseless optimism and doing so seems, however briefly, to be paying off: we reframe our hopes as entitlements. In the markets, it happens all the time, as any investment advisor will tell you. Half the job of a good one is managing the unrealistic expectations of private investors. With the crash of 2000, for example, technology stocks with their grossly inflated valuations got the blame, but people seldom discuss the conditions that made that possible. For years prior to that, ordinary people had been bragging over their back fences that they were seeing 20 per cent growth in this or that mutual fund, while investment advisors had been telling people to plan for their retirements on the basis of 8 per cent to 12 per cent annual returns from their retirement savings plans. Very quickly, numbers like that became normal in everyone's minds, reasonable even, to the point where people didn't even see themselves as gambling any more. In that state, they could easily convince themselves that Nortel was a bargain at a hundred bucks. They weren't trying to beat the game. They were just looking for their fair share of all that cake.

The value destruction that results from mob entitlement is, when you think about it, not that much different from the kind that happens at the mall, and I'm not only talking about stampeding Walmart shoppers. When we stumble onto a package of tube socks on sale for ninety-nine cents or a DVD player for $89, we don't feel lucky, we feel smart. What was really just good fortune in terms of our timing becomes our new normal. We don't think for a minute that our need for tube socks happened to coincide with the store's need to unload its excess inventory, or that this price reduction was the unimaginative marketing tactic of a share-obsessed scoundrel. By the time we reach the cash register, we've decided these are the true values of those products (and that anyone who paid more is a fool). The corporate cow, having no gift for debate or nuance, decides this is what works, shrugs, and finds a way to sustain those prices and still make a profit. Products get worse and, often, so does the process by which they're made. As everywhere in the universe, from Wall Street to the mall, when too many creatures want too much, everybody ends up paying, usually with interest.

Omaha's oracle has nothing but contempt for wishful thinking when it comes to value, especially if that thinking is coming from someone with a stake in the outcome of a transaction. In one trenchant passage of his 2009 shareholder letter, he criticizes the practice of corporations bringing investment bankers to the table when they're buying a company using shares rather than cash. He is incensed by how they can talk out of both sides of their mouths, how they can change their assessment of the value of a stock depending on who's listening and what reaction they're hoping for. If a company is going to buy this kind of advice from a hired "expert," he suggests, then the company should hire a second one to tell them why it's wrong. Failing that, his advice is, "Don't ask the barber whether you need a haircut."

And don't ask a bank how big a house you should have, or a car dealer how many options you can afford, or your prideful neighbour what you should pay for a DVD player. If you want to bend it like Buffett, the only truly reliable arbiter of value is going to be the one looking back at you from the mirror, and the only valid moment in which to judge it is going to be right here, right now.

———

Although I was a little disappointed not to find the famous *Charging Bull* sculpture on Wall Street, I was not the first person to think it belongs there. That was the artist's plan, too. The three-and-a-half-ton bronze sculpture was not a grandiose vanity installed in the Financial District for the amusement of the Masters of the Universe, as one might assume, nor is it remotely related to the bull in the Merrill Lynch logo. It was, in fact, a civic-minded prank. The sculptor, Arturo Di Modica, deposited it on the sidewalk in front of the New York Stock Exchange in the middle of the night on December 15, 1989. America, still reeling from the 1987 stock market crash, needed some cheering on, Di Modica figured, and *Charging Bull* was his gift. One night, with the help of some friends and a flatbed truck, he quietly installed the beast on Broad Street under the NYSE's Christmas tree, oriented so that it appeared to be charging northward toward both the Exchange and Federal Hall.

Shortly thereafter, the sculpture was confiscated by the NYPD and sat in an impound lot until the City was shamed by the citizenry into putting it back where the people could see it (you can now find it around the corner in Bowling Green Park). Fittingly, although it's now technically only on loan to the City of New York, it seems in no danger of going anywhere any time soon. Di Modica wanted to remind those who toiled there, and we can suppose the whole world, of "the vitality, energy and life of the American people in adversity." The power of the people is a message that never gets old. The corporation may be a cow, but the lethally brawny beast just around the corner from the heart of capitalism, it turns out, is supposed to be us.

The people who run corporations, the people who invest in those corporations, and the people who buy the products of those corporations are all connected. We all depend on our system of commerce to provide for us; we are all, indeed, in the same boat, all the time, however rancorously. But we also all face an ethical choice when we participate in this system, whether it's as shoppers or as investors or as capitalists: the choice between what we can get away with and what we can live with. The former option seems to produce higher highs (along, of course, with lower lows) and a simple, dramatic kind of win-or-lose narrative, giving capitalism the same sort of competitiveness that makes people stampede into Walmart on Black Friday. The latter choice, on the other hand, seems to produce something slower and less dramatic but more predictable and sustainable – something more about substance and less about chance, and if the Oracle of Omaha is any indication, something maybe even more successful in the long run. It's been said that behind every great fortune is a great crime but what seems to be behind this one is little more than a satisfied customer.

It certainly isn't for me to say which investment strategy makes the most sense. But if I had to bet on which one stands the best chance of creating a world we actually want to live in, my money would be on the farmer.

CHAPTER ELEVEN

BUYING THE CHANGE YOU WISH TO SEE IN THE WORLD

Naomi Klein's 2000 journo-lit opus *No Logo* wanted us to go to war. " . . . [B]uild a resistance," she writes in the book's final paragraph, "that is as global, and as capable of coordinated action, as the multinational corporations it seeks to subvert." Though her argument dressed its enemy up in the whorish attire of branded marketing, the book was really an indictment of bad corporate behaviour and an incitement to class struggle. "Taking aim at the brand bullies" was simply a clever way to get our attention and make activism personal so that it would haunt us every time we spent our money. Preaching from the gloomy left, Klein seemed to be saying that the system is inevitably corrupt and systemically broken and that our only hope is to abandon it altogether. *No Logo* came up short in terms of offering an alternative vision for how we ought to live, as these polemics often do. However, it was not short at all of suggestions about how to express our rage about it in the mean-time. As her argument unfolded, we were invited to protest, to subvert and undermine, to deface and defile, to "jam" the per-nicious culture of brands. What she proposed was little short of a resistance movement, a movement whose prime condition of membership was a willingness to opt out.

It didn't work, of course. Although the book sold exceptionally well and launched her career as a literary anti-capitalist radical, looking back on it a decade hence, the world she so reviles seems to have changed hardly at all. In fact, though this would be difficult to quantify, in my opinion the developed world is more branded than it has ever been, and most of us are pretty comfortable with that. Comfortable enough, at any rate, not to go to the effort of burning it down. Naomi, surely, is disappointed in the lot of us.

Whatever you may feel about the politics of anti-consumerism, such disappointment is what guarantees that no real change will ever come from this kind of radicalism. For a start, as I argued at the beginning of this book, staying away from the mall is the surest way to give up the power you have over our system of commerce. And protest of the placard-waving variety, because it's usually essentially neutral in its commercial consequences, is subsonic to the corporate cow. More than this, radical activism is alienating by definition. To buy into the arguments of the people with the pitchforks and torches, you have to first be willing to see the rest of us as stupid, morally weak, and easily manipulated, while at the same time being willing yourself to surrender some freedom of self-expression to their collectivist vision of grey moral superiority. This impossible paradox just shuts people down. Meanwhile, as you await this paradoxical epiphany, you are asked to believe that we – you, me, and everyone else we know – are, in fact, the enemy. One scholarly assessment of the phenomenon put it like this: "Viewed as hegemonically complicit in wrongdoing, yet manipulated and deceived by evil forces, the mainstream consumer and his or her view of the world are the main target of our consumer activists' ideology." In other words, anti-consumerist activism isn't even trying to win our hearts and minds. It wants to burn us at the stake along with the corporations to whom we stupidly give our money. That's why no good can come of it. It only offers us two alternatives, and both of them are ugly: we can either opt out of the system and thereby either destroy it or enable its faults, or we can opt out of the conversation and thereby ensure that nothing changes.

That's why, for the title of this chapter, I have gingerly appropriated the sage words of Ghandi. Economic non-violence might not just be the best way home, it might be the only way. The following stories about brands and consumerism, and the power to make change happen when you combine the two, prove it can work. These stories came about because people spoke as consumers with choices so that corporations had no choice but to listen. The leverage these people wielded didn't consist of angry signs and rattle cans of spray paint. There were no riot police with tear gas and there was no chanting, unless you count hungry kids in the back seats of minivans. Instead, as you'll see, the pitchforks and torches of the twenty-first century are our money, and our willingness to vote with it.

———

Back in the summer of 2007, HSBC in the U.K. did something that banks do all the time. They instituted a fee. It's the sort of thing that retail banks have been doing whenever it suits them since time immemorial and we, thinking of banks as somehow above the kind of market accountability that we expect from burger chains or deodorant makers, just accept it. Of all the consumer-marketer relationships, our relationship with banks is by far the most emotionally complicated. We hate them for the power they have over us, and we love them because we need their approval to make our way in the world. Banks, for their part, know this and have always taken our dependency on them pretty much for granted. Anyway, so much of what a bank does in the course of running its business is guided by regulations and balance sheets that the consumer, most days, is little more than an accounting line item and rarely a bank's main concern. It's always been understood that we need them more than they need us, which is hardly a recipe for empowered consumerism. If it's not forgivable, it's at least unsurprising that banks might feel entitled to take our money if they think they need it.

In this case, what the HSBC took away was an accommodation they had always given to their customers attending colleges and universities. In the past, students had been allowed to overdraw their chequing accounts without paying interest while in school and for a couple of years afterward. But one day, a calculator-wielding cow at HSBC decided that this accommodation was unprofitable and thus unnecessary. Henceforth, students would pay 9.9 per cent interest on their overdrafts. Serious money for a recent graduate. To make matters worse, many customers didn't receive notification of the change in policy until the first bill was practically in their mailboxes. So, besides being expensive, HSBC's new policy was also something of an ambush. Given that universities are petri dishes for radicalism of every imaginable kind, HSBC should not have been surprised that there was an outcry, but they probably weren't entirely prepared for the shape it took.

Aside from the more traditional expressions of protest that erupted, a National Union of Students (NUS) vice president from

Cambridge University named Wes Streeting put up something called a Facebook page. It was entitled "Stop The Great HSBC Graduate Rip-Off!!!" By his own admission, he didn't think it was going to be of significant tactical value for the NUS. He was just "inviting [his] friends on Facebook to respond, and it turned into a viral campaign." When the dust cleared, HSBC was shamed into reversing its policy for 2007 graduates and refunding the interest charges they'd billed them that summer. In a matter of weeks, mostly because of one ranty little web page on a social media site that had been available to the general public for less than a year, a giant global bank put the money back on the table.

In light of how common it's become for consumers and corporations to duke it out in social media, this story seems in hindsight to be encouraging but unremarkable. However, when you consider that this was 2007, it starts to look like something of a bellwether, bearing the hallmarks that would define every subsequent "viral" phenomenon.

For one thing, even going up against one of the nation's largest banks, it didn't actually take very many people to effect the change. At the height of the controversy, subscription to Streeting's Facebook page was somewhere between 2,000 and 3,000 people, none of whom were, as far as we know, especially wealthy or influential in HSBC's view. For another, it happened fast. This wasn't a matter of months of letter writing or years in court but just a few weeks between people receiving bank statements in July and HSBC waving the white flag in August. For yet another, the outcry was intensely observable. Within the Facebook community, there were customers who actually heard about the interest charges there first. People told their stories on message boards, angrily and personally, which made the impact of HSBC's decision more of a human than a fiscal one. The protest took on a life of its own, attracting the attention of the press. A bank charging 9.9 per cent interest was never going to be newsworthy on its own, but the reaction of a few thousand impoverished and betrayed young university graduates was.

Perhaps most important in the end, HSBC was compelled to make the first move. That was revolutionary. Campus radicalism in past generations had always meant taking physical possession of a space, interrupting and disrupting and retreating only when either forced to do so or when victory was won – that's what protest looked like. Now, the protesters just had to speak their truth where everybody could hear it, peacefully, and the enemy would be forced to come to them with a solution. "HSBC have contacted NUS to discuss this campaign," began the final entry on Wes Streeting's Facebook page. Victory had been won by wielding the simple power of public shame.

———

The story of the Apple brand is nothing short of mythic. Although the company's history strictly begins in the 1970s with a couple of plucky kids trying to invent the future of the personal computer in a garage, Apple's birth as a brand really took place in a commercial break during the 1984 Super Bowl. The brand's media debut very publicly – and extravagantly – proclaimed its intention to be everything the rest of the personal computer business was not. The now famous commercial, called "1984," portrayed users of its competitors' products as legions of soul-dead drones. Imprisoned by a system that exploited them as cogs in a techno-fascist machine, they appeared to be resigned to their fates simply because they had no choice. Now, Apple would liberate them. A beacon of feisty hope in an increasingly Orwellian world, Apple promised, "On January 24, Apple Computer will introduce Macintosh. And you'll see why 1984 won't be like '1984.'"

A cult was born.

Apple's myth only got better. Just over a year later, visionary founder Steve Jobs was cast out of the kingdom by a usurper in a boardroom coup, and dwelt in the wilderness for more than a decade (founding Pixar, we can suppose, as a way of passing the time). Darkness fell upon the land and the faithful were sorely tested, as, at times, were Apple's shareholders. Then, right on cue, came Jobs's triumphant return, and his vindication thereafter by win after marketing win, starting with the candy-apple-coloured iMacs, the iPod, iTunes, and on, and on, and on. It was a ripping yarn. The once and future king had done more than return his dominion to fiscal health. He had, it seemed, picked up right where he left off inventing everybody's future. The promise of liberation from the shackles of technological corporatism was being kept after all, and Apple's maverick army grew. Even the masses of it's-just-a-computer pragmatists who swore they would never be caught dead with one of the company's sleek machines inevitably found themselves with iTunes on their PCs and iPods in their briefcases. Maybe the future really wasn't going to be like 1984.

By the time Steve Jobs took the stage to introduce iPhone to the people of Earth in January of 2007, the audience at the Macworld convention was long past wondering about any of that. The energy among the assembled faithful in that auditorium was one of smug expectancy. Although the winsome little device looked different from anything Apple had done before, it was every inch the disruptive, brilliant, and slightly magical "reinvention of the telephone" (as Jobs modestly described it) everyone had been expecting. Jobs lovingly revealed each new feature of the iPhone as liberation for the people, and each one brought a fresh round of giddy applause. When the news broke, the lust to possess it, despite its steep $599 price tag, spread like a virus. When the iPhone was released for sale at the end of June that year, people literally slept on sidewalks in lineups that circled city blocks, just to be among the first to own one.

Boy, were they mad when, barely two months later, Apple dropped the price of the selfsame magical iPhone by $200.

The story's ending is deceptively anticlimactic. Apple had wanted, as Jobs would later put it in an open letter to customers, "to go for it this holiday season." That meant lowering the price of its product into a holiday gift-giving sweet spot. Obviously, it was not a popular move. There was predictable outrage from the faithful in the blogosphere, and plenty of media attention lavished on a pricing decision that nobody would have given a second thought to if the product at issue had been a toaster. Apple was soon compelled to contrition, or something close to it. In fairly short order, the company decided to offer $100 to everyone who had bought the iPhone at the original price. In Jobs's open letter to customers, he gently defended the price reduction as "life in the technology lane," but also offered a direct apology "for disappointing some of you," and added, "we are doing our best to live up to your high expectations of Apple."

As unremarkable as Apple's gesture may seem at first, this kind of thing doesn't happen very often. From video game consoles to sneakers, we routinely pay a premium for our impatience at the mall and then grit our teeth when months or even weeks later the same products turn up "on sale" in the junk mail flyers in our mailboxes. It's part of the game and when it happens we rage a little but eventually just accept it as the way of things. Given the normality of it, and given our own short memories for marketing outrages, it's a safe bet that Apple would have escaped serious damage from the episode had they done nothing. Given the particularly brutal competitive nature of the wireless phone business, the risk would certainly have been worthwhile for the benefit of placing a few hundred thousand more of these little money machines under Christmas trees that year. So why did they blink so quickly? Why the hundred bucks?

The answer is much the same as it was for BMW when Chris Bangle's design vision pushed the faithful too far. Apple was, in the end, a slave to its own cult. Its priceless brand had been built to its mythic proportions not by customers but by true believers. Central to their belief system was the promise that "1984 [was] not going to be like 1984," a promise that, in the quarter century since those words were uttered, had come to mean "why Apple will not be like ordinary corporate cows." It would be special. Different. It would be a champion of the creative human spirit, a brand that made money by making life better. As Apple's utopian vision unfolded in one product after another, those qualities transubstantiated themselves into the very beings of Apple customers, turning its products into conscious, very personal choices. Choices people would sleep on a sidewalk to be able to make. Those, in fact, are the real "high expectations of Apple." Those are the reasons that Apple owns the twentieth-most-valuable brand in the world, an asset estimated to be worth more than $15 billion all by itself.

When a brand stakes its claim on such high moral ground, it can't get away with very much. With an ambitious agenda of innovation still ahead of it in the years to come (its eyes were firmly on the media business by this time, with ambitions that are only just now becoming clear with the launch of its iPad), Apple needed people's faith more than it ever had before. The very same faith that had always made Apple strong also made it vulnerable, and the very same magic that allowed Apple to defy the conventions of its industry and still prosper also attracted the most unblinking scrutiny of its believers (not to mention a popular press more than willing to gleefully expose the brand's crooked halo to the world should the opportunity present itself). The bigger and more prosperous the company became, the harder those expectations were to meet with any credibility. We can believe a company is a principled maverick if it's determinedly small, but Apple wasn't that any more. It was growing fast – in May of 2010, the company's market value had exceeded even that of Microsoft – and its products were becoming ubiquitous. We can believe a company is a principled maverick if it does one thing passionately well, but Apple was stretching its brand across industries, becoming bigger and more transformational in the media world than it had ever been with personal computers. It was becoming corporate, and if it wasn't careful, it risked people seeing it as the very enemy it had been founded to vanquish. Its maverick brand credentials were disappearing. All Apple had left to keep the believers believing was its cult, and it only took the slightest twitch from those believers to remind Apple that its brand would always be their hostage.

That's the way it is with big, famous, valuable brands. The more they have to lose, the more fearful they become about publicly disappointing us. They usually don't warn you about this in business school, and people rarely say it out loud in boardrooms or at ad agencies, but it's at the very heart of branding's

Faustian bargain with the marketplace. Consumers look at brand names and see corporate vanities and empty promises, when what they should really see is the face of their own power.

———

Walmart can be a pretty arrogant corporation. As a customer, mind you, you might not see them that way. Their advertising is earnest and unpretentious and sometimes even cute. Their stated mission, to save us all money, is hard to oppose. Some people even love the store experience, which, despite the gargantuan scale of both the stores and the company, manages to remain somehow down-home and classless. Regardless of what we drove to get there, when we cross the threshold we are all one, careful with our money and taking more than a little pleasure in giving up as little of it as possible for the privilege of owning a branded product. A corporate mission of Walmart's was once said to have been "to give ordinary folk the chance to buy the same things as rich people," and what's not to like about that?

Some people think what's not to like is how they sometimes do it. Stories abound about their heavy-handed and dictatorial treatment of the companies that supply the products they sell, and how their determination to dictate pricing has driven manufacturers offshore or worse. Nonetheless, all in all, Walmart's way of doing business has produced an empire that would rival many of the world's nations in dollars and cents, and probably some of them in real estate, too. They're the largest private employer in America, and the world's largest corporation in revenue terms. The number of people who visit their stores in the United States is equivalent to almost one-third of the country's population. That scale gives them huge efficiencies, which obviously help them keep their pricing edge. It also makes Walmart very, very powerful. For many branded marketers, Walmart makes the marketing rules; for some of them, it is the decider of life and death. By extension, Walmart must be able to exert a great deal of control over what's available to us as consumers.

Limiting our choices is not something the corporate cow will do just out of spite, of course. It is something it will do, though, if it thinks there's money to be made, and the most successful retailers are ruthless about it. You see, the key to profitable retailing isn't just how much profit margin you earn on each widget you sell. The potential for profit is limited by the amount of shelf space you have to display those widgets, multiplied by how frequently you replenish that inventory. As a retailer, you'd rather make a buck each on something that sells a thousand pieces a day than make ten bucks each on a product that only sells ten pieces a day. Being very good at managing that is how you really maximize your profit in big retail. And Walmart is the best.

Keenly aware that this is a superpower of theirs, and keenly aware that even they might feel the pressure of recessionary consumer spending in the months ahead, Walmart decided in 2009 to cull the herd. Hundreds of branded products were "delisted" based on their sales velocity compared to category-leading brands, meaning that they would no longer be sold at Walmart. The valuable shelf space was filled instead with only the top-performing brands – the ones that sold at the fastest rate – as well as Walmart's own private label products, which even if they didn't yet sell at the same velocity had the virtue of higher profit margins for the company. Their competitive pricing would be preserved, they must have reasoned, while their profitability was improved.

Consumers would have a little less choice, sure, but that doesn't matter as much as a great price does, right? Especially not if times are tough. It must have seemed as if they couldn't lose.

In the aftermath, Walmart was uncharacteristically frank. Speaking at an investor conference in March of 2010, the company's Chief Operating Officer observed that, by eliminating choice, they had apparently "aggravated [their] customer." His first clue, I imagine, was that the fourth quarter of 2009 was the first time in the company's history that customer traffic had ever declined in their stores and the first quarter in which the company's sales had ever fallen. Industry sources showed that their market share in staple packaged goods products had dropped a little, too, meaning the problem wasn't that people weren't buying these products; the problem was that they were buying them somewhere else. That same month, marketing trade publications were reporting that Walmart was restocking three hundred branded items they'd culled in the previous year, and that this was probably just the start of a broader, longer process of restoring choice in an effort to win back those aggravated customers and, with them, the confidence of investors.

It had only taken a few months. Only a few shopping trips, for most families. The Goliath of retailers, one of the most influential corporations on the planet, was bullied by consumers into putting choice ahead of greed. And those consumers did the job by voting with their money. Rather than show up with slogans and signs and leaflets and burning effigies, they used the only language the corporate cow understands. They simply didn't show up at all.

———

The last story I want to share about brands and accountability isn't over yet. It may not be over for many, many years, nor is the outcome in any sense certain. But among its serious implications, for the ecological health of the planet and the energy policy of one of its richest nations, this story may prove to be a very telling test of what happens when a brand gives a disaster an identity.

When the Deepwater Horizon oil rig caught fire and exploded in the Gulf of Mexico on April 20, 2010, the first phones to ring with media calls were those of its owner, Transocean Limited. The Swiss-headquartered offshore drilling contractor was operating the rig, which was drilling but not yet in production when the catastrophe occurred. The rig had been leased to three companies for the work it had begun off the coast of Louisiana. In fact, there was a list of corporations with some kind of involvement in the project, including the controversial oilfield services company Halliburton. At the beginning, it must have seemed as though there was plenty of culpability to go around, and indeed a lot of the actors spent those first days after the explosion pointing fingers at one another. That didn't last long, though. In a matter of weeks, the Deepwater Horizon incident had a name: the BP oil spill.

The name shouldn't be surprising. Certainly, BP had the biggest stake in the output this well might one day produce, and certainly more of their money than anyone else's had put the Deepwater Horizon where it was, doing what it was doing. Watching the story unfold, though, complete with those garish disaster logos of which cable news networks are so fond, I couldn't help but think there was more to this decision to "brand" the spill this way. I couldn't help but think that, just as legions of anti-consumerist activists had done in the past with brands like Nike, putting a familiar name to the face of disaster would give people a way to connect with it, and give them a culprit who would be intimidated enough by their anger to take action.

· BP, you see, is unlike a lot of the corporations that drill and dig for minerals around the world. It has a consumer brand, and it's not just any brand, either. Theirs was, in 2009 at least, among the one hundred most valuable in the world, according to Interbrand's annual list. They've spent money and taken some risks to get there. The most famous of those risks, from the perspective of the marketing world, was the $7 million redesign of their logo in 2000. No mere act of corporate vanity, the logo's lovely green and yellow flower was presented to the world as a symbol of the oil company's commitment to environmental stewardship. The audacity of an oil company staking a claim on being green was startling and, from a branding point of view, admirable, if for no other reason than that it took some nerve. Yet their motivation was distinctly cow-like: "It's all about increasing sales, increasing margins and reducing costs at the retail sites," said then-CEO John Browne.

Ah, yes, the retail sites. What gives BP legitimate standing as a brand, as opposed to being just a corporate name and logo like Halliburton, is the fact that its logo adorns filling stations on street corners across the U.K. home market, Europe, and the United States. Every day, millions of people drive by them, and enough of them choose to pull in for a fill-up that BP pumps 22 *billion* gallons of fuel a year into American gas tanks at their 10,000 stations in that country alone. Multiply that times the price you paid for the last gallon of gas you bought, and you begin to see the size of the problem for BP. Few of us will ever decide to lease an oil rig, so the reputational – and thus economic – impact of a disaster like this on companies like Transocean and Halliburton will be muted, contained, and relatively short-lived. BP, on the other hand, has to face its constituency every day, one fill-up at a time. As I write this, the President of the United States has firmly asserted his conviction that BP is the responsible party, and talk of a BP boycott is becoming a dominant theme in news coverage of the disaster. Lists of BP's other retail products are being passed around on Twitter, and a boycott fan page on Facebook has, in just a few weeks, signed up subscribers in the six figures. The citizens of the consumer republic are manning the ramparts.

It very much remains to be seen what kind of consequences BP or the other stakeholders in this disaster – not to mention wildlife, coastal residents, and maybe all of us – will eventually pay. But that BP has been aware of what's at risk is unmistakable. Borrowing a page from the Tylenol playbook, BP's then-CEO Tony Hayward initially made himself the grim, weary, penitent face of the company with the press (as his insensitive gaffes in that role accumulated, it began to look more like he was volunteering for the job of scapegoat. If so, it worked. He was replaced in July 2010 and sent, literally, to Siberia). The corporation, meanwhile, reached beyond the immediate disaster to gauge its consequences; for example, writing a cheque for $25 million to the State of Florida to bolster its tourism advertising and reassure everyone that Florida is still open for business. At the Halliburton website's home page, the only mention of Deepwater Horizon is one of three rotating banners occupying about a sixth of the screen. At Transocean's, one column of information appears about halfway down the page, roughly equal to the space it gives its stock price. In both cases, if you want to know more, you have to click your way deeper into the site. Not so at BP.com. The entire home page is dedicated to the disaster, with latest news, contact information for the press and victims of the spill, a slide show of earnest-looking people working to solve the crisis, and a headline that doesn't say "BP oil spill." It says, "Gulf of Mexico response." BP is obviously frantic about plugging its gusher in the ocean floor on this day, but it is also assuredly frantic about its brand.

It seems much more than likely that government and the media were certain this would be the case, that the "branding" of this disaster was a deliberate strategy. Barely two weeks after the explosion, no less august an entity than the White House was putting BP's name to the crisis in public statements and on its official blog, where the crisis even had its own logo. The most marketing savvy American government in history knew, almost from the start, that neither law nor force of arms was going to get as much action as quickly from any corporation as the simple threat of destroying its brand. The strategy worked so well that it wasn't long before BP's very survival was being questioned, prompting President Obama to cool his rhetoric a little, saying, "BP is a strong and viable company, and it is in all our interest that it remain so." For the moment, at least, the BP brand was worth more to us alive than dead.

That small mercy only underscores that this United States government has apparently grasped, just as Naomi Klein did, that brands have all sorts of political utility. In the first few months of 2010, in fact, politicians made political hay by demanding that some of the most famous brands in the world be hauled to Washington, D.C., to account for their behaviour in the marketplace. Toyota, McNeil Consumer Products (makers of Tylenol), Google, and even Apple found themselves sitting in the glare of unwanted political attention for a variety of reasons.

It's debatable whether any of these companies ranks among the world's worst corporate villains – they almost certainly don't – but, as brands, they surely rank among the most powerful political statements a government so obsessed with the word "accountability" could make.

As for BP, time will tell. But it hardly seems debatable that branding this disaster was the best way to make sure something got done about it.

———

That "money talks" is one of those truths that is so fundamental it even predates consumerism itself. The proverb is mentioned in literature stretching back to the Middle Ages and has endured, altered less by the passage of time than by almost anything else we tell ourselves. Money's unmistakable voice remains a dominant currency of power in the world, and it's most certainly the foundation of our relationships with the corporations that try to sell us things. In the final analysis, the elementary particle in our system of commerce is cold, hard cash. We have it, they want it, and they'll do what they have to do to get it.

That means, of course, that we've always had a certain kind of power over those corporations. We've always had the option of denying our money to the hungry cow as a way to punish it for not giving us what we want, and of giving it to them to encourage them when they do. That's not a revelation. But, like most things from the Middle Ages, this kind of power is a pretty blunt instrument. To keep your money in your wallet or to change your mind about who gets it are the most unambiguous and costly signals a corporation can be sent. They're also a bit like jail: a useful but expensive last resort, unlikely to produce real reform, invisible to the rest of society, and very much after the fact of the crime. In the industrial age, when marketing was invented, our system of commerce was essentially feudal. As capitalism's serfs, we could take what we got from the corporations we dealt with, or we could rise up with our pitchforks and torches and put them bloodily out of business. We always had a choice, but it wasn't much of one.

Now, finally, that's all changed.

Marketers today rely overwhelmingly on their reputations to continue to do business. In the past they were fundamentally in the business of making things. They were obsessed with "differentiation," which then meant constantly inventing ways in which a product could be tangibly unique and a fresh object of desire. Brands were just the names they gave those products, and they were presented to us almost didactically through advertising in media channels that were few in number and corporate-controlled. Marketing as a process was focused on creating demand, which it generally did so well that retailers were grateful to carry the most famous brands and happy to boast about it. Desire was created by the marketer, and it was invested mostly in the products they made.

To be a marketer in the twenty-first century is to be an entirely different animal, one far more dependent on the value in brands. Many fewer corporations make their products in their own factories any more. Innovation is such a marginal thing that a great many of the products we buy could be fairly characterized as functional commodities. At a given price, most products aren't that different from their peers in any practical sense and few products are comprehensively bad. Retailers, many now powerful brands in their own right, encourage and enable brand substitution rather than fear it. In the moment we make our choices, it's far more likely that we're responding to the name on the label than to what we really believe is in the box. Desire has transcended practical benefit. Once upon a time, a corporation's fate rested on whatever was in its secret sauce. Now, it rests mostly on what we think of the company that makes it.

Meanwhile, it's become very easy for corporations to keep track of those reputations, and to do it in real time. There are so many more ways for us to be heard, so many more forums in which we can talk about what we like and don't, and about who has disappointed us. There are also many more surveillance mechanisms that allow corporations to hear us as we're doing it. They hear us directly, as when we speak our minds in a blog or on Twitter, and indirectly, as when we simply stop buying. A corporation can now see the change in its fortunes instantly. Instead of looking back at a quarterly sales result and guessing they must have done something wrong, corporations, if they care to do so, can both see the problem coming and know exactly what it is with a simple Google search. This gives consumers something we have never had before: the power to warn and threaten rather than to punish silently after the fact. There has never been much individual consumers could do to discredit a corporation's product, but today there is plenty they can do to harm a brand's reputation. Just as a democracy is impossible without a free press, so it is that an accountable marketplace is impossible without both brands and the means to talk back to them. Now, we have the power to do just that. Now, we can negotiate.

That's what makes opting out of the branded world such a futile form of protest. For one thing, it would be a shame to quit now, when the game is just getting good. To abandon our system of commerce just as it's become possible to affect it seems crazy. More than this, we've finally arrived at a moment in which we can actually teach the system *how* to change. We can remake it according to our principles, remake it in the image of our better selves, rather than having it shaped only by our urges. We can, in other words, give it a conscience. There's no question that if we want to save the world, we're going to have to go to the mall a little less often. But the real key to change is that now we can make it count when we do.

EPILOGUE

(In which capitalism acquires a conscience,
and everything works perfectly)

I really do have a broken toaster.

It was *designed*, the manufacturer's website informs me, in Europe; in hindsight, the cagey precision of that word should probably have raised my suspicions immediately. We chose the obscure brand because the toaster matched our remodelled kitchen, and accessories, as they say, are key. To be fair, it still toasts. What's wrong is more annoying than crippling: A part that is supposed to let you peek at your bagels to see if they're done without shutting off the element no longer elevates them. Instead, the lever flops uselessly, taunting us with the power we once enjoyed. It's made of plastic and it probably should have been made of metal. Probably not coincidentally, it was also made in China, in a factory that managed to achieve the brand's low manufacturing cost target for my toaster and still miraculously make a profit for itself.

I have no quarrel with cost targets, or with profit, or with factories in China insofar as I have never actually seen one. No, what rankles me is that I put some trust in the brand I chose. I figured that, if nothing else, their vanity would prevent them from putting their stylish logo on something that could ever flop uselessly. Now that I'm disappointed, I would have hoped they'd be a little bit embarrassed, in addition to correcting the problem. The fact that this product is branded was supposed to guarantee me that. Alas, they are no such thing. The warranty is up, which means that they don't have the option of simply taking it back and making me another one (in itself rather horrifying from an environmental point of view), so I have to get it fixed. Which, again to be fair, I can supposedly do. But you would be surprised at the number of appliance repair places that can't understand why I wouldn't just toss it and buy a new one.

And there, in one dull, trivial, all too familiar episode, is the whole problem. It's too easy to blame the marketer, or to blame Chinese factories, or to blame my own gullibility. That's a cop-out, as the hippies used to say. This didn't happen because I was stupid and the people who made my toaster were evil. It happened because people like me were disengaged and the people who marketed my toaster were opportunistic. It was this realization that made me finally understand the essentially political nature of marketplaces and set the stage for *Consumer Republic*.

We're taught from a young age that buying something is a simple value exchange: my money for your stuff. We think of these exchanges as discrete events, and we think of them as being rationally driven. But it's not really like that, is it? We take our money to the parliament of the marketplace dozens of times a week. We give it to whomever makes the most persuasive promise. Then we wait to see whether they meant it or not. Every one of those decisions is a vote. Every brand is a candidate. And every time we accept an unkept promise, or weak character, or bad behaviour, we effectively endorse it. The candidate learns the size of the gap between his stumping rhetoric and how little it might really take to win and keep the next vote. Just like a democracy, we're all in it together. And just like a democracy, we eventually get the toast we deserve.

———

For several years, I taught a university course called Strategic Brand Development. The students who took this course were people who planned to make their livings in the marketing world as creative communicators, one day finding employment in an ad agency, or a design firm, or a web marketing company. The essence of this course's syllabus was that a modern brand was no longer fully in the control of the marketer and couldn't (and shouldn't) be built just on the basis of clever tactics any more. Instead, it argued, the brands that are succeeding as businesses, and the ones that both marketers and consumers alike admire the most, are defined by some kind of purpose. These marketers operate as though they're on a mission in which they're going to make money by making someone's life better in some specific and valuable way, and their brands become constitutions that govern the way the organization operates. I wanted the students to think about brands not as superficial labels but as something a corporation should feel it has to live up to. A little idealistic, maybe, but what better time to indulge in idealism than in your third year of university?

The second session in the course outline was called "The Ethics of Branding," and it took the form of a free discussion. The purpose of it was to lay a foundation for the sessions to follow by getting the students to think about the role they were going to play in our system of commerce. Why are brands necessary? What do they do? What is the moral duty of the people who create them? That kind of thing. With any job, a person's performance and sense of personal satisfaction are going to depend mainly on how important they think their work is. The discussion was meant to put the students in touch with whatever calling had got them this far. They'd get more out of the course if they believed that their work matters.

Except they didn't.

With each fresh group, I would begin the course this same way, and each semester I was amazed at how cynical these young people were about the machine they were working so hard to be a part of. They were clear and vocal about their belief that branded marketing was exploitive and manipulative and at the root of much of what's wrong with the world, and they were tacitly but equally clear that they regarded the consumers who fell for it as indulgent fools. Although I could write a certain amount of this off to the inevitable left-tilting ethos of campus life, there was nonetheless little doubt that their ambivalence dimmed their passion for the study of branded marketing. It gave them a certain reluctance and cool detachment from the work they were in training to do. They weren't really buying it.

Psychologists call this "cognitive dissonance," the discomfort we feel when we're compelled to hold two conflicting ideas in our heads at the same time. Humans have a limited capacity for this, they say. It makes us crazy. Eventually, if we can't figure out how to evict one of the conflicting ideas, we'll adapt our values or our beliefs or our behaviour as much and in whatever way it takes to make the feeling of conflict go away. The cynicism of these students was just this kind of coping mechanism. These brilliant young people were creatively gifted and wanted nothing more than to make a living with that gift. But they were surrounded by a culture that not only believed that branded marketing was immoral by its nature but that it also didn't really have an effect on anyone with any common sense anyway. The conflict was between their passion for what they wanted to do with their lives, and the fear that it wasn't going to matter very much. So, to cope, they told themselves it didn't.

I wish I could tell them that this anxiety automatically dissipates when you get a job, but for many people it doesn't. The world of branded marketing is actually in a bit of a funk these days. There are pockets of fizzy optimism, yes, though most of these tend to revolve around the still-emergent Internet as a marketing frontier. But in much of this community, there is a sense that the job has devolved into a relentless battle just to stay even, and requires a steadily thickening skin to protect oneself from society's constant disapproval and the feeling that the best history has already been made. Inevitably, then, the marketer's cynicism deepens, too. He becomes the beast his consumers are suspicious he's been all along, and focuses his energy on finding a game he can win. Show me an airline that charges you for carrying your baggage, or a wireless phone company that rounds your call times up to the nearest minute, or a toy that turns out to be slathered with lead-based paint, and I'll show you a marketer that decided to serve the wrong master because the right one didn't seem important enough. Sure, greed explains much of this kind of behaviour, but it's hard to dispute that a cynical marketer begets a cynical consumer, and that a cynical consumer begets a cynical marketer. The sense that we're adversaries in this game is the real destructive force underneath it all.

This conundrum reveals yet another way that marketplaces work like democracies. Show me a corrupt, arrogant government, and I'll show you a low voter turnout; show me accountability among the people who run things, and I'll show you an engaged electorate. As separate as we may often seem or choose to think we are, we are locked in a codependent relationship in which we will constantly be looking to one another for cues to help us calibrate our own level of engagement. The question is, if we're going to change things, who has to make the first move? The answer, fair or not, is us. Because for all the power an elected official may have, he cannot ultimately choose his own fate. In our system, only we have that option, and that means we have to be the instigators. We have to be the ones who decide what matters. We have to show up, be heard, and, by conscientiously exercising our right to choose, declare our belief in the system. However imperfect the result, it will inarguably be better than it would have been if we'd stayed home.

In the parliament of the marketplace it's no different. When we look at the face of our own cynicism, we can't afford to see it as a sign that all is lost. We have to see it as an urgent call to arms.

———

At the beginning of this book, I asked you to think about the corporation not as an omnipotent, evil psychopath, but as a primitive, single-minded organism. A cow. A beast ploddingly bent on profit, and simply blind and deaf to everything that isn't either an enabler or an obstacle. I think it's a useful way for consumers to understand the companies behind the brands they buy because it clarifies what we have to do to get these companies' attention, to encourage the right kind of behaviour, and to punish the wrong kind. Conscientious consumerism is, in that sense, a sort of ongoing process of operant conditioning, whereby we teach and they learn by our using the only language they can understand. Brands give us power by creating choice and by requiring accountability; brands give them power by making their products more attractive, socially meaningful, and profitable. Brands are the fulcrum on which the whole system is balanced.

The most contentious aspect of this argument, I've been certain from the start, would be the idea that we, the consumers, are the ones who set the moral standard for corporate behaviour. The things that matter to us, expressed through the ways we choose to spend our money, become the parameters within which a corporation will operate, testing them only occasionally to see if they've shifted in some useful way. It's much easier to see the corporate world as both discrete from ours and as predatory to it. Yet the proof of our role in this is all around us. If we were each to make a list of the corporations that seem to have done the most harm in the world, the ones that seem to plunder with impunity, I'll wager that most of the names on most of our lists would not be those of soft drink companies, running shoe manufacturers, or people who sell plasma screen TVs. They would be the names of industrial companies, financial institutions, natural resources and energy companies, and the like. They would be companies shielded from our influence either because their customers are other corporations rather than people like you and me, or because they operate in monopolies and oligopolies or with patent or regulatory protections, whereby even if products appear branded, they actually offer us no real choice at all.

As it happens, there is a Swiss research company in the business of making just this kind of list, although not with any intention of defending the idea that brands create corporate accountability. It just kind of worked out that way. The company, Covalence, simply set out to rank the world's multinational corporations on their ethical track records. The index they've developed compares more than five hundred such companies, and was rigorously built, taking in seven years' worth of data on forty-five criteria that range from labour standards, to how the companies manage environmental waste, to their human rights records. While the pattern isn't absolutely consistent, it's hard to ignore that the companies ranking highest tend more often to depend on consumers like you and me to sustain their businesses. (Intel, HSBC, Marks & Spencer, Unilever, General Electric, Dell, and Procter & Gamble all made the top ten.) Or that the companies ranking the lowest are largely beyond the reach of our torches and pitchforks. (Of the worst ten, four are oil and gas companies, two are in "basic resources," and two produce industrial chemicals. The other two are a discount airline and a company that built its empire on cigarettes.) The further up the list you go, the more likely you are to recognize the brands and to find them in your closet, kitchen, garage, or office. The further down the list you go, the more likely it is – with a few startling exceptions – that you've never once seen them tagged for sale at the mall.

The Covalence study gets even more interesting when you take their list and compare it to Interbrand's ranking of the world's most valuable brands.

Despite the fact that Covalence includes plenty of industrial companies and conglomerates in its list – corporations that essentially have no brands – the overlap between its one hundred most ethical companies and the one hundred most valuable brands in the world is an eye opener. Fully one-third of the brands on the latter list for 2009 are among Covalence's top one hundred most ethical corporations for the same year, this despite the fact that Covalence's list includes corporations that Interbrand wouldn't even have looked at because they aren't global or don't sell consumer products. As broadly drawn correlations go, this one is hard to miss and not at all hard to explain. A mining company toils away in obscurity, accountable only to shareholders every three months and to unions and regulators only when something goes badly wrong. In contrast, those consumer products are running for election every week when you go shopping. They have to try a little harder and more constantly to stay out of trouble. Public accountability like this may or may not be a matter of corporate conscience, but it is most certainly good politics.

Consumerism, it turns out, has always been at its heart a political business. The power of self-expression that branded consumerism gives us is so potent that it has been considered the natural enemy of any sort of ideological totalitarianism. Whether you're trying to make teenagers behave in school or to subjugate a nation, removing people's right to spend money as they see fit and to display their choices is among the first tools of control any such regime reaches for. And, while there's no doubt it can bring out the worst in us, it also has a long tradition of instigating social change. Much as consumerism has sometimes enslaved us, it has also been emancipating, from creating a middle class to funding a free press. Determined and subversive, it is the most benign and yet public way we have of asserting our autonomy.

It's high time we started to think about our consumption that way. It's high time we separated the idea of branded consumerism from the excesses of its practice, respected the power it gives us, and put it to some more noble work. To abstractly oppose branded consumerism in all its forms, however moral that point of view may seem, is ultimately paralyzing. To blindly continue the pursuit of more stuff in a war of attrition with corporations will doom us all. The only conversation worth having, the only one nobody is having yet, is how to make it sustainable. How to gently slow down our system of commerce, make it more deliberate, and teach it what value means.

If thirty years of toil in the vineyards of branded marketing has taught me nothing else, it has taught me this: Nothing, no law, no force, no moral suasion, can move industry further or faster than the power of the choices we make. We just have to decide we're going to remake our marketplace in the image of our better selves – remake it in a principled way – and we can give it awareness and a conscience. In other words, we just have to vote with our money.

ACKNOWLEDGEMENTS

onsumer *Republic* was a personal mission and a joy to write. But this doesn't mean it was always easy, or that I wrote it alone. I was and remain lucky to have inspiration and help around me constantly. I acknowledge here a few of these angels, without whom I fear there might not have been much to say, or courage to say it.

My parents, Richard and Moira, deserve much credit for inspiring my way of thinking, as parents inevitably do. Depression-era kids, they taught me the value of a dollar, and what it should – and should not – mean for one's self-respect. This is the philosophical backbone of *Consumer Republic*. I'm also indebted to my students at OCAD University, who were the first people to demand that I defend the ethics of branding. You probably have no idea what a mark you left on me. To my friend Arkadi Kuhlmann, thanks for inspiration of another kind: That someone so immersed in the practice of capitalism still firmly believes it should not be a zero-sum game proves that good people can still play it. And thanks, too, to the City of

New York, where a good deal of *Consumer Republic* was written. I went there to see consumerism at its most intense, and instead the City and its people showed me humanity and an unbreakable faith in the possibility of reinvention.

I'd also like to thank the millions of people who populate the community called Twitter for their assistance in writing this book. This suburb of cyberspace may, indeed, be filled with quotidian trivia, but I assure the reader that it is also populated with smart, interesting, and generous people who are eager to share what they know. I am grateful for the integrity and diligence of my editor, Laurie Coulter, who was a worthy collaborator and a forthright, intelligent critic. As counterintuitive as *Consumer Republic*'s polemic is, nothing less would have sufficed. To my adopted "big brother," Dan Needles, and his wife, Heath, thank you for your fierce support, sensitive reading, and sage counsel about the writing life. You always knew exactly when I needed to hear, "This is normal." Endless thanks to my agent, Sam Hiyate of The Rights Factory, whose parsimonious praise and abundant faith kept me honest and got me this far. And thank you to the fantastic people at McClelland & Stewart, most especially Liz Kribs and Trena White, for believing in *Consumer Republic*, and for your partnership and professionalism.

I'm grateful every day for the love and support of my family. To my amazing wife, Linda Courtemanche, there are no words to explain how much I have valued your willingness to be a sounding board, your gentle early reading, and your incandescent sense of possibility. By sheer serendipity, my children, Elizabeth, Brendan, and Rafael, all in one way or another began their lives as autonomous citizens of the world while this book was being conceived and written. It was a gift to be reminded of the challenge and thrill of a new beginning. I am forever and always grateful for their love and loyalty.

B.P.
Creemore, Ontario
August 2010

NOTES AND SOURCES

In writing *Consumer Republic*, I wanted to capture the dilemma we face as a consuming society as it unfolded before us after the world's financial meltdown in 2008. To do this, I relied heavily on references from the popular media and on research that was current, circulating, and talked about in the marketing world as the book was being written from mid-2009 to mid-2010. By their nature, these real-time sources are, of course, prone to fallibilities, and digital content can change or disappear at a publisher's whim. What follows are notes on my sources for each chapter. Any errors and omissions are purely unintentional.

INTRODUCTION

The story of the 2008 Black Friday tragedy at Walmart in Valley Stream, N.Y., was well covered by the *New York Times*. Most of the report is from an article by Robert D. McFadden and Angela Macropoulos, November 28, 2008, entitled "Wal-Mart [sic] Employee Trampled to Death."

The impact of the Tylenol tampering incident on the brand's market share is widely reported with minor variations. These numbers align with my recollection of McNeil Consumer Products' version of the incident when I worked with the Tylenol brand in the late 1980s.

The Phillips study is cited here from memory. Like most market research, it was likely never fully published in a public forum and almost certainly not archived for future reference.

Data on the size of the world's beer market is from Wikipedia's entry on the subject, which includes a comprehensive list of citations.

The story of President Obama's "Beer Summit" was reported, among other places, in the July 30, 2009, issue of the *New York Times'* Politics and Government Blog. The piece, "What a White House Beer Says About Race and Politics," was by Peter Baker, Helene Cooper, and Jeff Zeleny.

Peter Stearns's quote regarding consumerism's historical link to freedom and individual choice is from his book, *Consumerism in World History: The Global Transformation of Desire*, Routledge, 2001.

Quotes and references to Naomi Klein's *No Logo* are from the 2000 Knopf edition of that book.

The assertion that Nike was not as focused on social responsibility in the '90s as they are today is partly from memory and partly based on a comparative review of the content of their corporate website in those years. That site's indices and some content survive more or less intact on the Internet Archive's "Wayback Machine."

Nike's ranking among the world's most ethical corporations comes from ethicalquote.com, a corporate ethical performance monitor published by the Swiss research company Covalence.

CHAPTER 2

The television shows mentioned in the comparison between the 1980s and 1990s were selected from lists of top-rated prime-time programs for each decade, kindly supplied by the Nielsen Company.

Douglas Rushkoff's quotes come from his book *Coercion: Why We Listen to What "They" Say*, Riverhead, 2000.

The comparison of Porsche's and BMW's sizes is based on worldwide vehicle sales as reported in the companies' annual reports for 2009.

The chronology of Chris Bangle's career at BMW is sourced from the Wikipedia entry about him, which includes a comprehensive list of citations.

The blogger quoted in the story about Starbucks' opening a store in New York's Lower East Side is Deanna Zandt. The piece, entitled "The Starbucks Tipping Point," was published on the blog alternet.org, August 8, 2005.

CHAPTER 3

Television audience numbers are from the Nielsen Company.

Historical cost comparison data for advertising on the Super Bowl are from adage.com, whose original sources were Nielsen and the television networks rate cards for the years in question.

Steve Ballmer's 2009 address to the advertising glitterati in Cannes is available on the festival's website, canneslions.com.

The shift of advertising spending to on-line media was reported on forbes.com in a piece by Dirk Smillie, titled "A $65 Billion Advertising Shift?" and published July 21, 2009.

The increase in corporate spending in social media was reported on aspnews.com in a piece by Kenneth Corbin called "Social Network Ad Spend Surging," published September 24, 2009, again relying on Nielsen data.

CHAPTER 4

The Thorstein Veblen quote is from *The Theory of the Leisure Class*, as transcribed in the Gutenberg Project's on-line edition.

The rules regarding recycling of automobile content in Europe are from the End of Life Vehicles Directive, Directive 2000/53/EC of the European Parliament. The complete legislation is available at eur-lex. europa.eu.

The percentage of Porsches still in service claim is as made by the manufacturer.

Lifetime fuel cost data for the 2008 Jeep Wrangler and Toyota Prius are from CNW Marketing Research Inc.'s "Dust to Dust Automotive Energy Report."

The story of the Toyota Tacoma buy-back was widely reported. I have used information from an article by Christopher Jensen in the *New York Times* entitled "Toyota Offers to Buy Back Rusty Tacomas," published in the paper's on-line edition, May 7, 2008.

The Gallup data on confidence in the Toyota brand was reported by Gallup, Inc. in a news release March 2, 2010.

CHAPTER 5

The refrigerator comparison data is from J. D. Power's 2009 *Home Appliance Study*, which is reported on their website at jdpower.com.

The information on Samsung's share of appliance retail showroom space is from IFR Monitoring's *Shelf Share Report*, quoted in *This Week in Consumer Electronics (TWICE)*, February, 2009.

The Adam Smith quote is from *The Theory of the Moral Sentiments*, originally published in 1759 and transcribed on adamsmith.org.

Quotes from Dr. Elizabeth Suhay regarding her Social-Emotional Influence Theory come from the abstract of her thesis and from interview correspondence between us for this book. I am very much in her debt for her enthusiasm and generosity with her time and intellect.

The quote from Yankelovich, Inc.'s white paper "A Darwinian Gale" was published on their website, yankelovich.com, in November 2009, to promote the study to corporate clients.

CHAPTER 6

Dr. Grant McCracken's work with the Royal Ontario Museum is briefly described in his book *Plenitude: Culture by Commotion*, Periph:Fluide, Toronto, 1997. I quote the book in this chapter. Grant was kind enough to confirm my recollection of the details and support my interpretation of its ultimate implications in correspondence between us for this book. Insights from his original work on the anti-smoking campaign for Ontario's Ministry of Health are summarized in a presentation called "Smoking Cessation Ethnography," which can be found on slideshare.com.

The Rushkoff quote comes, again, from his book *Coercion*.

Comments on the 2010 U.S. Census are from an article by Bradley Johnson called "New U.S. Census to Reveal Major Shift: No More Joe Consumer." It was published on adage.com on October 12, 2009.

Alessandro Jacoby's quote comes from correspondence between us during the research for this book. His 5brand experiment continues at 5brand.net.

Three published rankings inform my comments on brand value, admiration, and trust: Interbrand's 100 Most Valuable Global Brands, *Fortune*'s 50 Most Admired Brands (rated by business people), and *Business Week*'s Most Trusted Brands (rated by consumers), all for 2009. All are published by their creators on their respective websites.

CHAPTER 7

Quotes about the end of carefree spending, and my observations about the pragmatic optimism of American consumers in the midst of the recession, come from the 2009 Met Life Study of the American Dream.

The remarkable Stephanie Nolen's commencement speech is quoted as it was reported in the *Globe and Mail*, May 22, 2009, and is used here with her kind permission.

Neil Boorman's story is fully told on his website, bonfireofthebrands.com. The toilet paper quote comes from an excerpt that appeared in the *Guardian*, August 25, 2007.

Colby Buzzell's article, "Digging a Hole All the Way to America," appeared in *Esquire* in August 2007.

I quote Dave Bruno from a blog post dated December 29, 2009, on his blog guynameddave.com.

CHAPTER 8

The *Wall Street Journal* article, entitled "Spendthrift to Penny Pincher: A Vision of the New Consumer," was written by Lisa Bannon, and published on wsj.com on December 17, 2009.

China's overtaking of Germany as the world's largest exporter was widely reported. I refer here to an article by James Thompson in the online edition of the *Independent*, which appeared on January 11, 2010.

Comparative economic data was observed from tables published by the Organization for Economic Cooperation and Development (OECD) on its website, oecd.org.

The relative happiness of Europeans versus North Americans is widely reported. My source here was an article by Graham Hill entitled, "Europeans Happier than Americans Yet Half the Footprint," which appeared in the *Huffington Post*, June 24, 2008.

Comments on the history of consumerism in Europe and quotes are again from Stearns's *Consumerism in World History*.

Observations on the apparently disparate values of various European nationalities are from "Beating the Recession: Buying into New European Consumer Strategies," published in April of 2009 by the McKinsey Global Institute.

Comments on the French attitude toward money are from *Sixty Million Frenchmen Can't Be Wrong (Why We Love France But Not the French)*, Jean-Benoît Nadeau and Julie Barlow, Sourcebooks, 2003.

Data comparing the working hours of Europeans to those of Americans comes from an article entitled "Counting the Hours" published by the OECD Observer at oecdobserver.org, March 2008.

A wealth of examples of the persuasive power of reward in advertising can be found at vintageadbrowser.com.

Comments and some data on the differing attitudes of Europeans and Americans towards work are informed by a draft abstract for the article "Why Europeans Work to Live and Americans Live to Work," by Adam Okulicz-Kozaryn, Institute for Quantitative Social Science, Harvard University, which was published on-line April 12, 2009. (Since I conducted my research for this book, the full article has been published on-line in the *Journal of Happiness Studies*, under the title "Europeans Work to Live and Americans Live to Work [Who Is Happy to Work More: Americans or Europeans?]"; DOI: 10.1007/s10902-010-9188-8.)

Comparative data for living space in Europe versus the U.S. come from a report called "The EU vs USA," prepared by Fredrik Bergstrom and Robert Gidehag in 2004 for the Swedish libertarian think tank Timbro.

CHAPTER 9

The "United Breaks Guitars" story is retold mostly from Dave Carroll's own version, published on his website, davecarrollmusic.com, with the chronology supported by various news sources and the Twitter stream from the days following the video's posting to YouTube.

The Nicholas Negroponte quote comes from the introduction to his book *Being Digital*, Vintage, 1995.

The Eric Schultz quote was originally reported in *Advertising Age* in a piece by Nat Ives, and Google was kind enough to confirm its accuracy for me.

John Battelle's comments are from a conversation and correspondence with me during the course of researching this book. I am in his debt for giving me the time, and for being so incisive with what must have seemed to him pretty basic questions.

Rahaf Harfoush's comments are also from a conversation and correspondence with me during the researching of this book. She, too, was generous and incisive, and if her intelligence and passion for the subject are representative of her generation, our future is in very good hands.

The quote from a Democratic Party supporter regarding President Obama's position on FISA comes from a post to the campaign blog, mybarackobama.com.

The blogger who wrote about the Obama campaign "entering completely new territory" was Micah Sifry, in a post to personaldemocracy.com on July 3, 2008, entitled "The FISA Protest and MyBO: Can we talk? Can they listen?"

The "intense backlash" quote comes from a *New York Times* piece by James Risen entitled "Obama Voters Protest His Switch on Telecom Immunity," published in the on-line edition July 2, 2008.

The information about the number of corporations active in social media comes from an article in *Fast Company* by David Pakman, called "How Social Media Is [sic] Upending the Enterprise," published in the on-line edition October 1, 2009.

The story about IBM's social media surveillance product was reported on mashable.com May 11, 2010, and the product is explained more fully in an IBM corporate press release available on ibm.com.

The reference to how corporations use Twitter comes from a study called "The Global Social Media Check-Up," published by the public relations firm Burson-Marsteller in February 2010.

The sobering datum regarding North Americans' years of on-line experience comes from internetworldstats.com.

CHAPTER 10

My use of the phrase "Masters of the Universe" refers to Tom Wolfe's characterization of a Wall Street bond trader in his book *Bonfire of the Vanities*, Bantam, 1987, and not to Mattel's media franchise of the same name.

The 2009 annual report of Berkshire Hathaway, Inc. is quoted extensively in this chapter. I want to disclose that at the time of this writing, I owned some stock in Berkshire Hathaway. References to the investment practices and the character of Buffett himself are made here simply to challenge the notion that conscientious consumerism and successful capitalism are not necessarily at odds, and not to endorse Buffett's firm or his investment philosophy.

Warren Buffett's wealth ranking and net worth are from the annual list published by *Forbes* as it appeared on forbes.com on March 10, 2010.

Buffett's common stock holdings obviously change from time to time. My observations are from a list that was published May 7, 2010, on buffettbuys.com.

References to brand valuations are based once again on Interbrand's annual ranking.

The data regarding stock market performance for companies that invest in brands comes from a report entitled *Credit Suisse Identifies 27 Great Brands of Tomorrow*, published by the Credit Suisse Research Institute on February 25, 2010.

Data regarding the reputations of American corporations and Americans' intent to buy from and invest in them comes from the Summary Report of the 2009 Annual RQ Study by Harris Interactive Inc.

The "useless, self-serving windbags" comment comes from a piece entitled "Please Hold for Mr. Buffett," written by Buffett's biographer Alice Schroeder for *Business Week*'s March 8, 2010, issue. It may or may not be a direct quote from Mr. Buffett, but it was not reported as such.

The "what life should be about" quote comes from the legendary George Lois speaking in the film *Art & Copy* (2009).

The wonderful story of the Wall Street bull is anchored in a piece by Robert D. McFadden for the *New York Times* entitled "SoHo Gift to Wall St.: A 3 ½-Ton Bronze Bull." It was published the morning after Di Modica's gift was discovered, December 16, 1989. The quote from the artist's pamphlet was verified for me by author Fran Capo, who researched the story for her book *It Happened in New York City*, Globe Pequot, 2010.

CHAPTER 11

Naomi Klein is once again quoted from *No Logo*, the 2000 Knopf edition.

Comments on the folly of anti-consumerism come from "Adversaries of Consumption: Consumer Movements, Activism and Ideology," Kozinets and Handelman, published in the *Journal of Consumer Research* in December 2004.

The essential facts of the HSBC story are from the web edition of the *Guardian*, August 25 and 30, 2007, and from the Facebook page, which is still live.

Video of Steve Jobs's presentation of the first iPhone at Macworld is available on YouTube.

At time of writing, Jobs's open letter of apology and rebate offer can still be seen on apple.com.

Apple's brand valuation is, once again, from Interbrand's annual list.

Walmart's mission "to give ordinary folk the chance to buy the same things as rich people" is not officially a matter of marketing record. It was confirmed for me by a Walmart insider, who indicated that the corporate mission has since been rewritten.

Data about the size of Walmart is from the company's corporate website.

The story of the product delisting was reported in a piece by Jack Neff entitled "Walmart Reversal Marks Victory for Brands," published in *Advertising Age* on March 22, 2010, and quotes are from this article.

Background on the ownership and operation of the Deepwater Horizon are from CNN's coverage of the explosion in the immediate aftermath, April 21, 2010 and represent the facts as they were understood at that moment.

The story of BP's corporate logo redesign was reported by the BBC on July 24, 2000, and the quote from the former CEO is from that story.

Information on the size of BP's U.S. retail operations comes from the corporation's website.

The reference to President Obama's assertion of BP's culpability was specific to the press conference he held on May 27, 2010.

The information regarding BP's financial support for Florida tourism comes from an article by John Kennedy in the *St. Augustine Record*'s on-line edition, May 18, 2010.

The White House blog item I refer to was posted to whitehouse.gov/blog on May 5, 2010.

President Obama's comment about the importance of BP's viability was quoted in *Bloomberg Businessweek*'s June 28–July 4, 2010, issue.

INDEX